Jada Pinkett Smith

Biography

Life, Career, and Talent

PETER V WEINGARTNER

TABLE CONTENTS

"No, I'm just resting my eyes," he said, not even attempting to open them. A small smile appeared on his face.

Our daily lives were orderly in my grandmother's home. Having certain tasks to complete made me feel like I was contributing. They were difficult, but they were never dull. Marion Banfield understands how to transform the banal into magic.

In retrospect, I can see that she was growing two gardens. One of them was her backyard garden. My garden was her other garden. Grandmother poured all she had into my cultivation, growth, and learning, just as I saw her pour everything into her garden soil. Literally.

My grandmother's garden served as both my school and playground.

I spent countless hours outside in that backyard, either by me or with my relatives when they came to visit. My imagination taught me how to enjoy myself completely on my own. One of my favorite solitary games involves constructing a bustling fictional restaurant on the stone steps that separated the garden's two tiers. There was plenty of soil for making mud pies with weeds I collected and then decorating the tops with flower petals. Dandelion mud pies became a home specialty.

Marion was always a role model for hard effort. Her point was that even the most simple tasks, such as weeding, demanded thought and effort. Grandmother was a tightwad. She adored a spotless home, as do I to this day. I'm not exaggerating when I say I was taught how to clean a house from floor to ceiling. Cleaning the bathroom entailed more than just scrubbing sinks, tubs, and toilet bowls. Scrubbing and cleaning every inch of porcelain, including the cracks at the base of the toilet, was a PROCEDURE.

The greater lesson was that how you dedicate yourself in minor daily tasks is how you will apply yourself in big life responsibilities. I learned everything Mom threw at me, including cleaning, washing windows, setting and emptying tables, and doing dishes, pots, and pans. It was all about paying attention to details when it came to cleaning, but those floorboards had to be spotless. To this day, I am terrified of a white glove.

My grandmother's house had no spanking policy. There will be no tickling either. We were also not permitted to play hide-and-seek. When challenged, Grandmother pointed out that spanking or striking children was akin to experiencing the horrors of slavery. Tickling has long been used to torture prisoners of war in various civilizations. She disliked hide-and-seek because, as she recounted, "I was once scared out of my mind when someone who had been hiding behind a door jumped out at me."

Nobody dared to challenge her house or her rules.

Marion was exceptional in more ways than I can count, but she was a lousy cook. She enjoyed making her own foods, which sounded terrible when she described them and were even worse when served: Crock-Pot braised cow tongue with sour cream comes to mind. If Pero, the enormous black standard poodle I adored and rode like a pony, had been allowed near the kitchen table when we ate, I could have sneaked him the food I didn't want. There was no such luck. If I didn't complete my dish, I'd be eating it the next day, and the day after that if required. My grandmother did not engage in food waste.

Marion was a never-ending source of intrigue for me. She was a well-known socialite in the community. Forest Park Senior High School named a library after her, and Fallstaff Middle School named a garden after her as well. She was outspoken and remained active in the civil rights struggle throughout her life; she was a prominent role in Baltimore politics. So much so that she became the chair of Kurt Schmoke's campaign when he successfully ran for Maryland's first Black state's attorney, paving the way for him to ultimately become the city's first Black mayor.

Grandmother enrolled me in tap dancing, piano lessons, and, not long after, tennis, gymnastics, and anything else looked enriching. She urged me to read great children's literature like Alice in Wonderland, Roll of Thunder, Hear My Cry, The Learning Tree, and Gulliver's Travels. My reading was part of a summer school program she designed specifically for me since she believed I could have fun during the summer while also learning. There was no such thing as a break from school.

Not everything she came up with made sense to me, but one thing was certain: my grandma adored me. And it was pointless to fight her will since I would lose. So, when she later chose to run an after-school program at my middle school to teach students flower arranging, I went with the flow—sort of. My internal monologue went something like this: Who does this?

Except when I was in first grade and was scolded by a dance instructor for being unruly in class, my mother rarely interfered with Grandmother's curriculum. To emphasize her point, the teacher changed me from my pink tutu to a black tutu and placed me in a corner facing the wall.

My mother became enraged when I informed her about the incident and approached the teacher. My mother couldn't believe the woman had the gall to punish the only Black child in her class by forcing her to wear a black tutu. My mother had no problems in making the point in her angry Adrienne tone, which is still a sign to get out of the way. To add gasoline to her anger, it turns out that my mother was also put in a corner for being chatty in junior high school. Marion had gone to the school as soon as she heard about it. Adrienne was not only enraged at the kind of humiliation I had endured, but putting her foot down was in her blood.

That was the end of that ballet class, as you might expect.

Grandmother never told me about the horrors of racism she seen and experienced. She was usually upbeat about social progress for Black people and discussed how we might assist and inspire one another. Her idea was that a child's mind should be nurtured with optimism so that as an adult, they would work for change. Yet she was equally convinced that knowing your history was critical.

As a result, in January 1977, she broke the unbreakable rule of my eight p.m. bedtime. This was for the miniseries Roots, which was based on Alex Haley's seminal book of the same name.

I sat by Marion's side for the entire eight episodes, spellbound. My reactions were complicated—both fascinated and perplexed. That massive black chain around Kunta Kinte's neck, and the pictures of victims being lashed until they bled, stuck with me. Even though it was terrible to watch, my grandmother felt it was necessary for me to be a part of this historic event—the unprecedented major TV broadcast of a pivotal period in African American history.

Whereas Marion was active in Dr. King's "combat hate with love" campaign, my mother and aunt Karen grew up waving Black Power fists. In any case, taking a position against injustice was instilled in me at a young age.

Marion identified as an atheist, but her purpose was to expose me to all religions and ideas in order for me to find meaning for myself. She had no faith in organized religion, but she had a strong belief in one guiding principle: love. She thought that the Ethical Society, where we attended meetings every Sunday, was the right place for us to learn love and acceptance. At the time, it was unheard of for a Black West Indian family to refuse to attend church. We were meant to be somewhere in a Baptist church. Marion, not so. When it came to her truth, the status quo was out the window.

Grandfather, Grandmother, and I would ride in our yellow Volvo, which both of my grandparents thought was the safest and most trustworthy car on the road. The meetings of the Ethical Society were held at a humble home not distant from us.

We'd walk into the house to find seats lined up for a morning lecture, complete with a podium in the center, as was customary. We'd sing songs about the winds of change and peace and listen to different speakers talk about how understanding and love can bring humanity together. Later, the children would be moved to a smaller room upstairs to study about various religions practiced in various places and nations.

Meetings of the Ethical Society exposed me not only to the doctrines of Christianity, Judaism, Islam, Hinduism, Buddhism, and other faiths, but also to their followers' histories and cultural customs. It was enthralling to hear about distant cultures and the customs and rituals that conveyed the enigmatic communion that believers discovered with their understanding of God.

Those Sunday gatherings shaped me into a lifelong seeker of spiritual truth. The more I learned, the more I realized that all religions have great information to share, but they all share one essential belief: God is love.

Jesus, Allah, and Buddha could all be paths. But the truth was that the Higher Power will make itself available based on the needs of each particular soul. It became my firm belief that the Higher Power, whatever you call your Source, resides within the temple of your heart.

Of course, at such a young age, I lacked the vocabulary to express these thoughts to my grandmother. I just knew that my heart and mind were free to roam in that location because Grandmother chose to take me there.

Chapter 2: Leaving the Garden

Bullying became an issue in second grade.

There was this large boy with the crooked teeth who wouldn't leave me alone. He yelled at me one day, "You better bring me ten dollars tomorrow or I'm going to beat you up."

What's ten dollars? What am I going to do with 10 dollars?

I took the money from a location where my grandfather stored cash out of desperation.

Grandmother was originally APPALLED when she received the call from the school. There had to be an error. But when I told Grandmother the incident, she understood I must have been quite scared to steal money from my grandfather.

Marion Banfield concluded that the school could have done more to prevent the situation from escalating. Every child, in her opinion, should feel comfortable at school. Her recommendation was that I attend a private school.

I wasn't sure because I'd come to the conclusion that there was a significant gap between how I was educated at home and how I was educated at school by this point. The traditional structure did not suit me.

My mother thought I was a total failure in school. She was adamant that I should be at a school with Black teachers, Black principals, and Black students, which was nearly impossible in private schools. But she was willing to look into alternatives for my sake.

Marion set up a trial with a Montessori school so they could evaluate me. My first assignment was to write and illustrate a short tale. It sounded like a good time! I chose to write a narrative inspired by the authors I read on Mommie's bookshelves, such as Stephen King.

Such books were not entirely appropriate for my age, but I had always enjoyed horror and ghost stories. So I made one in which someone was stabbed in a cave by an unknown monster and provided a drawing. Even though I was overjoyed, the teacher conducting my interview was disturbed. I wasn't protected from bullying at first, and now I'm being misunderstood by grownups who don't know who I am. No, there is nothing wrong with me, and you folks are incorrect.

Was Stephen King flawed in some way? He was a genius, no doubt about it.

Despite being accepted, I did not stay at Montessori for long. Mommie and Marion thought I needed more structure because, strangely, I went from being bullied to ruling the show at this school. All I wanted to do was play, chat, and tell the teachers what I was going to do and what I wasn't going to do.

Another posh school was our next target. The one-day trial there wasn't bad, but I wasn't used to being in an all-white environment and felt like an alien.

I informed Mommie right away, "I don't like it here." Thank glad I wasn't given enough time to demonstrate how awful I was.

Mommie and Grandmother then agreed on a happy medium: Mount Washington Elementary, a public school with a diverse teacher and student body. This school was not far from Grandmother's neighborhood, and even closer to Uncle Leslie's, Aunt Marsha's, and Cousin Tiffany's friendly home, where I walked every day after school.

The situation had improved, but it was far from perfect. Because I was little, I was constantly picked on by both guys and females. In fourth grade, a much bigger girl approached me on the playground and, for no apparent reason, grabbed a chunk of my hair and yanked so hard I thought she'd take it out by the roots.

Aunt Karen was there when I came home to Grandmother's house that evening, and I told her everything and asked if she might come to school with me the next day.

Karen had the gleam in her eye that I occasionally saw in Adrienne. "Don't come in here telling me about some girl pulling your hair," she remarked. If someone touches you, be certain they do not do it again."

I kept my voice low.

My aunt Karen was stunningly beautiful and equally tough. She had no choice. My aunt and mother were both always trying to prove in school, "Don't let these looks fool you." Karen had been through a few abusive situations, including having her jaw smashed by a boyfriend (who Adrienne chased down with a baseball bat) and having her son, my cousin Brett, taken away by an ex. I'll never forget hearing my aunt yell for her child, my one-year-old cousin yell for his mother, and my mother yell at the cops to intervene. Aunt Karen had no idea where Brett had gone for two years.

As a result of these experiences, my aunt Karen and mother carried the burden of "I'm not to be played with." The ghosts of their anguish and the roots of their violence left their imprints on me, allowing me to defend myself when necessary. And by default, I learnt that whatever violence I could muster would prevent me from—my pain. Both physically and emotionally.

Karen's remarks have stuck with me. Of course, if I could, I would avoid a fight, and I never went looking for one. But as I grew older, fighting became an unavoidable aspect of survival, and if someone wanted to put me to the test, I had no issue answering the call.

Adrienne's love of music, all sorts of music, was one of the lasting gifts she offered me. And that love became ingrained in my bones. Mommie listened to R&B, pop, a little rock, disco, and even country. Kenny Rogers was her favorite musician. It was a fiesta on Saturday mornings when we cleaned our living area in the attic. Teena Marie's "Square Biz" or Cheryl Lynn's "Got to Be Real" infused the air with enthusiasm. Mommie ALWAYS had a record player, no matter where we lived. Mommie collected vinyl records, and vinyl became my passion, to the point where I planned to buy my own LPs as soon as I could obtain a job. Prince was my first buy.

Going to watch Raiders of the Lost Ark with my mother was a spur-of-the-moment decision. I was nine, almost 10, yet I was unprepared for the awful, horrific visions emerging from the ark.

My grandma wasn't thrilled about getting up and preparing her chaise couch for me to sleep on, but she didn't abandon me. Even if it contradicted her rule that children should never sleep in rooms other than their own. It didn't escape my notice that she made an exception and let me sleep on her cherished chaise.

During this time, Grandmother began to weave in reminders on the need of not relying solely on a husband or any guy for assistance. "Always have your own money," she said several times. "Do not depend on a man for financial security." She was very open about the birds and bees, telling me as a child, "Know how to enjoy yourself." Your enjoyment is yours alone, not a man's."

Maybe my grandmother was preparing me for a moment when she wouldn't be here. Nobody ever mentioned anything to that effect. In my opinion, she was going to live indefinitely.

The major event of the summer of 1981 provided me with a new sense of independence. I was already a latchkey kid, walking myself to school every day, riding my bike everywhere, and having free run in the neighborhood as long as I got home before nightfall. This summer, I got a taste of California's streets. Mommie had arranged for me to fly out to California to visit Rob in his new home. He had a new wife, a newborn son named Caleeb, and a stepdaughter named Regina, who was a few years my senior.

It had been an adventure. Palm trees and blue skies, as well as CUTE lads ranging from tall chocolate drops to lowriding cholos. I went from flying out in my tidy ponytail, dressed in a pretty little gown designed and made for me by my grandma, to traveling home to Baltimore in some Rick James-style cornrows with beads and everything in a matter of minutes.

That hairstyle transformed my life! I felt like a genuine adolescent like Regina. I like waving my hair and hearing the beads CLICK-CLICK-CLACK against each other.

Mommie unexpectedly announced her engagement to Tony not long after I returned from California. They'd been dating for a while, and the three of us were heading to the courthouse to make it official.

Mommie looked at my face to see how I was reacting. I didn't try to hide my dissatisfaction. We were not looking forward to sharing space with anyone other than my grandparents. I was used to it being just her and me, and despite the fact that she had a string of lovers, they had never moved in. Furthermore, they were never around frequently enough to advise me what to do.

Was I going to have someone pretend to be my father now? And I'd have to compete for Mommie's time and attention? Nope.

My mother was so overjoyed and certain that this was the proper thing to do that I accepted the fact that I had no say in the issue. I'd just have to deal with it.

All I could do was smile and be as courteous as I could while standing in that courthouse posing for photos. I didn't want to ruin

14

my mother's celebration, but I couldn't help myself. Through all of the smiles and romantic "I dos" and "forevers," all I could think was, "We'll see."

We had the least fun doing homework, but he rose to the occasion—a perilous task, because I was a struggling, easily frustrated student. English, social studies, and anything slightly related to creativity were all straightforward. Math, on the other hand, made no sense. Although I could add, subtract, divide, and multiply, arithmetic word problems irritated me. As a visual and tactile learner, I couldn't grasp an idea by being told how to grasp it; you had to demonstrate it to me. Tony was both patient and consistent, but it didn't change the fact that I wasn't.

We almost always got along, but every now and then, we had a traditional father/daughter dispute that really irritated me. Every day in middle school, a boy taller than me and much thinner than me mocked and bullied me. When he yelled at me, I tried to remain calm and reported him to my professors. There was no action. Then, one day, in the library of all places, this jerk got in my face while pushing me beyond my physical limits. His pointed finger came dangerously close to my nose. That was all I needed to jump on him. I went FULL RED, as if possessed. All I remember is the library aids yanking me away from him.

We were summoned to the principal's office right away. The youngster had significant scratches on his face and neck, which the principal interpreted as indicating that he had all of the injuries and that she needed to come down on me. I had already lost countless fights in elementary school and had the scars to prove it, but not this one!

My principal was actually quite nice. I thought she was reasonable. But she was mistaken in this situation. Nobody was going to convince me that I didn't have the right to defend myself. That's what

I'd been told.

This encounter served as a learning experience for my subsequent journey as a mother. It taught me not to oppose a child's determination. Any of my children would most likely have strong willpower, and when the time came, I promised to fight for understanding with patience rather than breaking their will. And God blessed me with not one, but three children who are fiercely independent.

At the age of twelve, I had an experience onstage that convinced me that performing could be my calling. It was part of a summer program. This time, I'd been cast as Dorothy in The Wizard of Oz.

As I recall, the house was crowded. My mother and grandmother Marion were there, as were Tony and many of my family members who had come to support me. I was overjoyed.

And just as I was about to fly into the last solo of "Somewhere Over the Rainbow," I realized I'd forgotten the words.

It was a moment when I could have fallen apart and wrecked the entire concert. I may have decided to leave the stage for good. Instead, I used my confidence, resolve, and discipline to declare, "I have forgotten the words to the song." Why don't you join me in singing them?"

They succeeded. It was as if the scene had been carefully orchestrated. I felt like I was casting a spotlight on the audience, which everyone enjoyed. That became one of my happiest moments, because I made sure the event went on without a hitch. It was an intensive lesson in the power of "Don't let 'em see you sweat."

My desire to perform became more serious after that. I had already started attending an after-school program at Baltimore School for the Arts called TWIGS (To Work In Gaining Skills), which was considered a stepping stone to getting into the performing arts high school.

Miami Vice premiered on Friday nights just before my thirteenth birthday. Tony and I watched every episode together, speculating on stories and marveling at the fusion of the old cop-show framework with the latest MTV styles and scenes.

Those Friday nights were magical while they lasted. They quickly came to a standstill, however. The world was suddenly no longer safe.

The knockout blow arrived in early 1985. Even though Marion had been ill for some time, it never occurred to me that she may not be with us—with me—at some point. She had previously survived cancer, and when it resurfaced as bone cancer, I expected her to do so again. Grandmother was just seventy years old, so she was still pretty young.

The family was probably in the same state of denial that I was. Marion kept up with the holiday and birthday parties for as long as she could. I recall one of the final Christmases we spent together. Marion invited Shirley and Grant Pinkett to Christmas dinner with the Banfields for the first and only time. It was as if she realized the significance of closing the circles and making complete peace that year.

For all I knew, everything in the world appeared to be in order.

Until my uncle Leslie arrived to fetch me up from school one day. This was quite odd and immediately gave me the impression that something was awry. When I approached him, he gently informed me that Grandmother had died. I could only say, "Okay." A part of me thought he was mistaken, because my grandmother's absence seemed unfathomable.

I noticed my lifeless grandmother lying on her bed as I stood outside her bedroom door. My granddad was broken yet doing his hardest to stay together. My mother had just arrived, and she was distraught. I was paralyzed by grief's confusion.

"Come in closer so you can see her, Jada," Karen gently encouraged.

I took three more steps in and resolved not to go any further. At that point, I had to acknowledge that it was a relief that all of her anguish from bone cancer, all of her wailing and discomfort, was done. She appeared to be at ease. I accepted that my grandmother was no longer present in what appeared to be a shell.

All I could think about was how death could be so cruel and not allow me to say goodbye.

Tony and Mommie filed for divorce shortly after I lost my grandmother. In less than six months, everything of the firm earth beneath my tiny feet vanished. Tony gave it his all. He told me that despite his and Mom's divorce, "you are still my daughter."

Unfortunately, his assurance faded quickly, more or less after he met a woman who tried to be maternal toward me at first but gradually barred him from contacting his ex-wife's daughter. I'll never forget receiving a phone call from her and hearing her say, "Find your real father," before hanging up.

She tormented my mother and me nonstop until Grandmother Shirley called her. Shirley informed her that she knew people in high places and that if she troubled us again, she would ruin her life. We never heard from that woman again, but I also never heard from Tony.

Chapter 3: The B-more Streets University

By the mid- to late-1980s, Baltimore had earned a reputation as one of the country's most hazardous inner cities per capita. This was especially true for children my age, fourteen and fifteen, who were among the most likely in the country to be murdered by their peers. It became the usual for a guy to be killed just by stepping on someone's brand-new sneakers. Or refusing to part with their dookie chains or leather puff jackets. Don't imagine for a second that girls are immune to violence. In a family argument, one of my homegirls was stabbed to death with a kitchen knife.

Hair salons seems to be a typical location for males in a jealous frenzy to murder their partners. We were also jacked if we were in the wrong place at the wrong moment. Let's not even get started on the drug trade and the heinous killings it inspired—we'll get to that later. Not every street or block was a combat zone, but there was nowhere you could go without being on watch. This was true of the row house on Price Avenue that Mommie and I resided in following her divorce—a row house she was able to purchase with a little down payment. Despite the fact that it needed a lot of maintenance, it was flanked by attractive working-class homes.

This was my new normal. This was what we were given, and the streets of B-more served as an initiation. They certainly prepared me for my future in unexpected ways. If you were young and Black, you had to make your way through the streets. If you let it, the curriculum at this university will set you up to fail. The necessity to survive was unavoidable. But that wasn't enough for me. In my mind, I needed to figure out what it took to thrive. The University of the B-more Streets appeared to provide opportunity, a way to make it big and, for some, to be at the top. I went out on the streets in search of my come-up.

I was probably the last of my girlfriends to lose my virginity when I was fourteen, not long after Marion died. I recall girls in middle school having sex with adult men. We all grew up quickly, wild'n out in ways that our parents never suspected.

How did I do it as the sole child of a street-savvy young mother? For one thing, Adrienne was plunged into a state of severe sadness in the aftermath of her mother's death and her divorce from Tony, which drove her to become a full-fledged heroin addict. She didn't have anyone to answer to, no one to hold her accountable. What's more, guess what? There was no one holding me accountable because of her addiction. During her graveyard shift, there was a lot of trouble for me to find. On top of that, danger always seemed to find me when I was just minding my own business.

Although my enthusiasm for self-expression lent itself to a variety of other pursuits, acting was always the thing that I excelled at and seemed to be a plausible career path. I would attend every dance lesson I could whenever possible. You name it: modern, ballet, African, or jazz. I, too, was a fan of the visual arts. Because voice, like movement, was such an important aspect of the actor's arsenal, I was able to obtain vocal instruction as well.

I was fortunate to have a unique person who inspired me to realize my own possibilities early on. Donald Hicken was the theater department's head. Donald was gentle but forceful, eager to go to bat for me when the occasion demanded it. But there came a point when I was sure I was testing his patience—after he turned the other way too many times as my attendance record deteriorated. At that point, I went missing, along with my classmate Cory Washburn.

We hadn't gone missing at all. Cory and I had just decided to travel to New York City since another BSA classmate, Josh Charles, was living there as a full-fledged working professional actor with his own apartment and everything. This was after he had a brief part in the John Waters film Hairspray, which was shot in Baltimore, however his breakthrough film role would come a little later, in Dead Poets Society. It sounded like a good idea to go to New York and hang out with Josh and learn how to get a real-deal job in show business.

I got behind the wheel and drove back to Price Avenue without incident. Except for... I had no idea how to parallel park. In a hurry, I drove back to Warren's house, forcing him to accompany me as I parallel parked the rental car and took the subway home.

Phew.

I found Cory, packed and ready, inside Baltimore's Penn Station, and we went to buy our tickets. Our Amtrak train was soon chugging along to New York City's Penn Station.

What transpired after that is a bit of a blur. We had a good time for a day or so, hung out with Josh, and wandered the big-city streets like we'd met celebrities. The school then called my mother about my absence that day for whatever reason. They had never done this before, despite the fact that I was always missing school. I'm not sure why they chose that day.

There's nothing like walking into a popp'n club at fifteen or sixteen years old, no ID required, and feeling like you own the place. It's dark and brooding, yet it's full of potential.

But my attention was drawn to the dance floor, and at Club Fantasy, as at other clubs such as Signals, Godfrey's, and Odell's, the music was what set it apart. Local acts such as Miss Tony, a drag queen ("How U Wanna Carry It" and "Pull Ya Gunz Out"), were popular in Baltimore at the time.

Hearing any of those songs would always get me pumped up for the dance battles.

On the floor, I had no qualms about going after the boys who were dominating the matches. I'd spin in with some hip-hop mixed with house routines, moving from Running Man to the Cabbage Patch, till I'd arch my back into some African dances I learned at BSA, pounding my feet as my torso twisted from right to left. As the audience began to applaud, I'd throw in some modern dance, a few pirouettes, and finish with some house footwork, while jokas attempted to outdo me. Even if my moves weren't always the best, I was a performer whose showmanship was unrivaled.

I eventually established myself as a dangerous dance battle threat.

I seized every opportunity to perform. Dance battles were followed by lip-synch competitions, where I was able to pull off a really fantastic Prince impression, which led to local and even national talent events.

These were very memorable times.

I'm grateful to have grown up during the early days of hip-hop. Rap music has always been about fusing influences that aren't represented in mainstream music. MCs were required to bring their own unique approach to the mike, as well as smart rhymes. What I liked about hip-hop at the time was that it provided an avenue for rebellion with an Afrocentric focus, providing us with education about our Black heritage that we couldn't obtain anywhere else. Our history classes in school were a farce. We weren't learning anything about our ancestors, societal inequities in our communities, or our lineage in African civilizations. We couldn't even comprehend the whole extent of slavery, so we had to rely on hip-hop geniuses like Rakim, KRS-One, and Public Enemy, Sister Souljah, the X Clan, MC Lyte, Queen Latifah, Salt-N-Pepa, Sugar Hill Gang, Grandmaster Flash, Poor Righteous Teachers, and others. They instilled pride in the culture.

Rappers were also giving a middle finger to the systemic hurdles that told us we were unworthy of equality and success through their rhymes. And that resistance echoed along our streets via our speakers. The messages varied based on who was rapping, and the more unique your presentation and delivery, the better your chances of cutting through the crowd. Women rappers that rose to prominence in my teens were incredible. They could hold their own against any male rapper and then some. In contrast to the misogynistic language that would soon dominate hip-hop, their rhymes delivered themes of female empowerment. They taught us to be proud of our voices, lives, and bodies.

Prince's style, both in clothing and music, was daring and unapologetic from the outset, and he won me over as a lifelong fan. And he was a manly male who dressed up in makeup and high heels. His high-pitched whines and screams were a captivating contrast to his baritone vocals. Simply lip-syncing to songs like "I Would Die 4 U" or "Let's Go Crazy" was exhausting. I could only imagine how it felt for him to really do them. Prince was one of the first artists I saw who demonstrated the thrilling beauty of fusing disparate worlds and energy. He demonstrated that they could not only mix, but were also required to produce something new and different.

Every type of narcotic was present in Baltimore, but heroin reigned supreme. Beginning in the 1970s, narcotics poured a flood of cash into the largely Black communities of every major metropolis. It was also a time when legitimate occupations that used to sustain families and connect communities were disappearing, with large companies closing down and leaving less opportunities for working-class people, young people, and so on. Many people would turn to the drug trade to make ends meet, to make a fast buck, or even to sustain their own habit. Because there was so much goods flooding metropolitan communities, practically everyone was connected— selling, purchasing, or utilizing. In the mid-1980s, a cheaper variant of coke known as crack began to gain hold in Baltimore, claiming to be far more addictive than cocaine itself.

The concept of gaining some financial freedom by selling drugs just sounded sensible to me—making a way for myself in a world when so many terrible things were happening. With my warped reality, selling drugs seemed normal and not as dramatic as the daily horrors—like the time one of my homeboys was shot several times and left dead in the middle of the street from one a.m. until seven a.m. the next morning. I'll never forget the sound of his mother and sister sobbing in the streets as they stood by his body all night.

When the morgue refuses to come to that section of town to reclaim the body of a young guy stolen by violent gunfire, a certain type of silence falls over the area. When one of its own is left to decay on the concrete under the midnight sky, the hood has its own way of mourning and paying its respects.

This was real life, and it was nasty and unfair. The only thing you could do was win—by whatever means necessary. Is that self-centered? Yes. But that was just for survival. When you live in an atmosphere where you are perceived as inferior and feel unworthy, you will treat others similarly. These kinds of dog-eat-dog situations may render anyone selfish, and selling drugs may become just another aspect of life. This was my path to financial independence and mobility. I had no intention of becoming a hustler's girlfriend. I'd witnessed firsthand the extent of control and servitude that comes with being financially dependent on a man. Some of the girls in my network looked to their drug-dealer partners for places to stay, vehicles, jewelry, and clothes, but at the expense of experiencing cycles of betrayal and abuse that were inconceivable to me.

Screw that. It was going to be me who provided myself with the trappings of the good life. I concluded that I could be just as successful as any other drug dealer. In my opinion, I could eventually work my way up to running an entire operation—be a queenpin.

The truth is, I didn't want my hands bound by anyone, and I certainly didn't want my hands tied by the system. Strivers a generation ago, like my grandfathers and Tony, became doctors and attorneys. The most prosperous people in my neighborhood were now drug dealers. They had the life that we all desired. It might be yours as well if you were strong enough and could endure.

My mom came in so high one day when I was at my part-time job at Merry-Go-Round that I couldn't believe she had managed to drive to the store without an accident. She wanted to put a leather trench coat on layaway for my birthday.

I'd never felt embarrassed in public by her before, but when she started talking to the guy who managed the store—who she knew and had come over to say hello—and nodded off standing up, I felt that shame.

"Ma?" I shook her arm; she opened her eyes and took a deep breath, dug into her purse for the money to put down on layaway for the coat, and pretended to be fatigued after a long night in the hospital.

Nobody spoke to me after she went. I made no attempt to describe what we had just seen. We all knew what it was, and there wasn't a single person in that store who hadn't been affected by the addiction crisis. Even though I knew I wasn't alone, it didn't make the situation any easier. Seeing her illness in the solitude of our home provided a false sense of normalcy, but I couldn't deny the gravity of my mother's addiction in public. Something was clearly wrong with her, with me—with both of us.

My resentment didn't manifest itself until an incident involving one of Mom's boyfriends. Adrienne had always been cautious about inviting males into her home, especially after her divorce. That changed when she met Anthony, the quintessential tall, dark, and attractive type who also happened to be a full-fledged heroin addict. He was frequently in our house, and items began to go missing as a result.

At one occasion, a shopping bag containing new clothes and money went missing, and my mother remarked that she couldn't find my grandmother's necklace, which she shared with my aunt Karen. Our next-door neighbors notified my mother that they had observed Anthony enter the house through my bedroom window and leave with some goods. When my mother confronted Anthony, he admitted to stealing from us in order to obtain drugs.

My mother was devastated. She made Anthony apologize to me, but what shattered my heart was that my mother felt it was alright to let him back into the house since he had apologized. I was surprised, feeling angry, vulnerable, and ignored. My personal space had been invaded. If I couldn't feel safe in my own home, I couldn't feel comfortable anyplace.

That was the second I realized I needed more control over my life. I could get back any money and clothes he stole. No worries, I reasoned, I'm not going to trip. This act not only justified my drug dealing, but also fueled it.

Why? Because I needed to get away. I didn't want to be a part of it, but I couldn't leave my mother behind. That's a huge conflict.

I'm not sure how I got into slinging marijuana. I recall there being a lot of hustlers at the skating rink, and I began developing relationships with the lower-level males whose egos were waiting to be stroked there. I caught my first fish on some "I need a mentor" nonsense, someone showing me the ropes because I wanted money.

M (we'll call him M) initially asked if I wanted to do a drop for him.

"Naw," I said. You should give me something on the arm, and if I treat it well, we'll go from there."

I was certain I didn't want to be a mule. I didn't want to be in a situation where a guy had his boot on my neck. Mules were never in charge. I wanted to be in charge.

M smirked and looked at me for a moment. I don't think he took me seriously, but he did want to make me and himself laugh. He finally laughed. "Aight, shorty."

He handed me a small gift to get me started. I quickly worked my way up to BP (we'll call him BP). He was an attractive midlevel hustler who taught me how to handle a gun, how to protect myself, and eventually assisted me in getting a job in Cherry Hill where I could sell dope out of a first-floor apartment window. I was soon introduced to Chet, who was on his way to become a kingpin and would eventually serve ten years in prison.

The first thing Chet taught me was how to be low-key, as in no expensive automobiles or jewelry. The second rule was to always have a legitimate job. The third need was that I devise a strategy.

Chapter 4: Advanced Degree

Pac's excellent looks didn't truly grab you during our adolescence because his sculpted features and everlasting handsomeness hadn't fully arrived. Even in tenth school, he had pure, undiluted charisma that was out of this world. At first, what he saw in me could have been simply that I was the cute feisty female in the room. That's the initial move for any curious masculine spirit—wanting to know her name and discover what's going on. Basic.

And yet, all I can say is that our immediate connection, I felt, went beyond the "basics," and this is what drew me in. From the minute we met, we were inseparable. We were like spirits in so many ways, and while Pac had an attraction to me at first, the more time we spent together, the clearer it became that there was no romantic spark between us... at all.

Being as young and as close as we were, we both found it perplexing that we weren't romantically attracted to each other. As a result, the day he got on my last nerve about being more than friends, I dared him to kiss me.

Pac grabbed me in his arms without hesitation and did precisely that. The kiss lasted only a few seconds before we both backed away in disgust. It didn't feel right. Pac drew back, his eyes squinting as if he had sipped rotten milk. "What the fuck?" he murmured as he wiped his lips.

I burst out laughing. "See! "I warned you, dummy!"

Our alliance, however, was not without its difficulties and consequences. We were both ferocious, passionate, and dangerously obstinate. This resulted in wild battles. We didn't take each other's crap, and we also knew how to harm each other like no one else. Between us, our tongues were the sharpest of blades. These fights could leave us unable to communicate for days, if not weeks. But we were always able to return. Always.

Pac and I became closer, and I found that, like my mother, his mother, Afeni, struggled with addiction. His surroundings, like mine, were unstable and chaotic. We genuinely bonded as a result of riding the same roller coaster as our mothers and experiencing the same sorrows and frustrations.

I took some things I'd purchased him to school early in our friendship—several shirts and a jacket. But I had to exercise caution. "Yo, Pac," I said as I began to show him my buy. Gap was having a sale, I believe. So, I was acquiring some items for myself when I saw this badass jacket and couldn't help but think of you wearing it. "I thought to myself, 'This would be fly as fuck on Pac.'" I pressed the jacket on his chest. "Damn! "I was correct."

As he clutched the jacket's corners, the largest smile sprang on his face. "Yoooooo! After all, you're not such a jerk. This is insane!" He proudly put on his khaki jacket.

Pac was unconcerned with their folly. He was dedicated and well-known for his daring rap battles. He could freestyle and rhyme you into submission when he was fifteen or sixteen. We were each other's biggest fans, giddy with delight as we watched one other accomplish what we loved. I like watching his rap bouts, and he enjoyed watching my dance battles. The inevitable moment arrived when Pac tried to persuade me, "You should rap." Jada, you'd be awesome!"

"I don't know, Pac."

"Come on, come on!" Stop being a prick! "I'll make you a rhyme."

Pac was adamant about having a female rap battle squad, and I couldn't say no. He gathered me and two other girls and soon organized a rap battle for us. Pac made me rehearse my rhyme with him every day after school. I WAS AWESOME. Pac genuinely tried, saying, "Listen to me," and then reciting the rhyme for me.

Could you imagine? Pac's cadence and style were as exciting back then as they were when the rest of the world first heard him. And here he was, attempting to make me rhyme like him. Pleeeasssse! He just assumed that my inability to do so was due to my stubbornness. Pac would say, "What? Is your great-great-great-grandmother white? Are you coming through now? What is your tempo? Are you listening to the guitars or what? Square, go on the beat!"

I was never able to find my cadence. But I persisted in the fight, and we prevailed. I made it out alive without too much embarrassment for Pac, but my rap career stopped there.

John Cole was a BSA visual artist who was rarely on campus. I got butterflies every time I saw him. I was so taken with him that instead of simply introducing myself, I asked two friends to do so in the lunchroom one day.

When John stared at me, it felt as if his eyes were piercing into my soul. He was emotionally open while being elusive. He remained to himself and his paintings most of the time, and I could sense a gentle yet wounded heart in him.

He wasn't my usual choice for male beauty—I preferred Black dudes, or street dudes, to be precise, and John Cole was neither. He was the polar opposite, pale white with white-blonde hair all over. White blond, not yellow blond. To some, he might have appeared almost transparent. But, in my opinion, he was... stunningly handsome. His face and body appeared to have been fashioned like one of those ancient Greek statues. He was unique, and I was drawn to him.

We all experienced some kind of dysfunction and trauma in our lives, but Pac's background was so tainted by poverty that I believe he felt the strains more acutely. Pac stayed with his mother and his adorable newborn sister, Sekyiwa, in a temporary extension at the back of the house.

He collected what he needed, motioned to the front door, and then led me to meet his mother. And there was Afeni in the dark, following Pac across the extremely motionless and heavy emptiness.

As I got to know Afeni, I realized she inherited many of Tupac's characteristics. Afeni was bright and well-educated, and once she made up her mind, she couldn't change her mind. She had a smile that could light up a room, and when she started talking about anything she was passionate about, it was impossible to look away. Pac was identical in every way. All of this common magic might occasionally be the source of conflict between two very intelligent, strong-willed spirits who were already embroiled in their own personal problems.

And I turned to leave, trailing Pac out of the home.

I never returned to that house after my first visit.

The closer we got, the more John confided in me about his sadness, which had to do with his mother's crippling stroke and how it had stolen the mother he previously knew from him. Pac and I had both lost our mothers to substance abuse. All three of us were orphans in some way. Our mothers had died in various ways.

In the best possible way, we were codependent. We'd strive to make up for each other's losses as much as we could. What the three of us were going through became the glue that held our friendship together forever. I had discovered a new garden.

Being with a young man as intensely passionate as John was liberated. He brought that enthusiasm to everything he did, from the music he liked to his drive to help people to his art and the way he loved. He was likewise enthusiastic in sharing all aspects of life with

Pac and me. He'd occasionally accompany us to Odell's on North Ave. and lie in the cut as I dance-battled. He'd later explain that he rarely got to see me dance since I was constantly surrounded by a sea of people, whereas he stood as the only white person among a sea of hustlers. He was unconcerned. He was always up for a game of kickball with Pac and me, no matter where we were.

No topic was off-limits in our shared universe. Pac, who was fiery and articulate, preached political lectures to me and John, paying special attention to the condition of the Black community. It was at these impromptu gatherings that I learnt about the Black Panther Party (his mother, Afeni, was a former Panther) and the teachers who created its ideology. Pac taught me a lot of history that I had never known before, and he talked about how that past was still influencing the systemic misuse of power in efforts to destroy Black communities.

In these moments, I had a glimpse of how Pac could transform the molecules in the air around him in ways that the rest of the world would soon experience through his music, movies, interviews, and, most importantly, his presence.

In my own research, I discovered that there were still holes in both groups' thinking that held Black women back—because we were ultimately expected to bring Black men ahead. Pac and I had many heated conversations about sexism in the civil rights and Black Power movements, as well as the absurdity of how Black males fighting for their independence and autonomy had a tough time thinking their women deserved the same. This was always a source of frustration for me, and Pac and I would argue about it. Pac adored women, particularly Black ladies, but he had his reservations. I could go as hard as he could, but when he hit me with some powerful realities, I was more willing to give up my need to be right. Pac didn't give up his urge to be correct that easy, but man... I knew how to put him down. We both enjoyed our cerebral and intense discussions.

John was both our audience and our learner at times. One day, as John and I were shopping in a store, I became aware, because to my newfound radical awareness of racism, that a white female clerk had been eyeing and discreetly following me.

He was incredibly sweet, but we both realized that he would never have such experiences. I knew this would cause a schism between us, no matter how hard he tried to understand. That made me wonder if I could ever seriously accept white men as love partners. It was terrible enough that most Black men didn't comprehend the struggle of Black women, but to contend with a white man who, no matter how hard he tried, wouldn't be able to get it? Which was the worst?

John was able to see beyond these things. He worked with spirit, which dissolved obstacles and filled gaps. Things simply were. I was impressed by his ability at such a young age. No, I did not.

For the time being, however, I had found some solace in the company of these two extraordinary and accomplished guys. Both of whom loved me for myself in different ways.

By the summer of 1987, various facets of my life were colliding.

The fact that I was transitioning from occasional low-level dealing to more frequent selling made it tough to keep my worlds separate. John, who was persistent, wanted to be with me in my various worlds. Even as a bright, almost iridescent white person in the center of settings where he had no business, he wasn't afraid or daunted. His lack of fear made me nervous. I told him repeatedly, "Listen, you can't accompany me everywhere... You can't be sneaking up on me like that. "I'm going to be where you can't be." He didn't understand. He would simply disregard what I said.

Aside from John and Pac, I had homegirls who treated me like sisters. Nonetheless, unlike many female social groups, my pals and I rarely posse'd up. Each of my girlfriends represented a distinct flow and offered me different levels of connection to something important that I needed.

Toni, my skating partner, had recently relocated from New York to Baltimore when I met her at the rink. She was tiny, like me, and had a laid-back personality. It didn't hurt that she could SKATE her a$$ off, making them an ideal match for learning tricks and showing off. My other pals didn't skate, but Toni and I couldn't get enough of it. We experienced many experiences as well as some misadventures.

Fawn, my girl, and I spent a lot of time together. She was tall and gorgeous, much like her name, and a little older than me, with the freedom to move with me whenever/however she pleased. She was quite quiet and smooth. She knew no one and didn't want to. Because I trusted her, she was the girlfriend who probably knew the most about my drug habits at the time. She didn't ask questions, so if I got a page and said, "I've got to make this stop real quick," she just nodded and we rolled.

Fawn's family, like mine, struggled with addiction. Our loneliness and bleak family circumstances were frequently alleviated by each other's companionship. We were both free to come and go as we wanted, and Fawn was always up for anything.

Then there was Ramsey, who studied visual arts at Baltimore School for the Arts. Ramsey, who is half-white and half-Japanese, has a significant Japanese ancestry on her paternal side. Being mixed racial created a unique relationship with her white maternal family, who raised her. In other ways, she was orphaned as well. I was able to watch the bigotry that Asian American women encountered via Ramsey, which was extremely different from the racism I faced as a Black woman. What she went through had various nuances and complexity, but she was just as troubled by white supremacy as I was. This was especially true because she lived just across the street from some KKK members.

My homegirl Keesha, who also attended Baltimore School for the Arts, was one buddy I couldn't take anywhere since she preferred to stay at home. Geraldine, a dead ringer for Sade and soon-to-be entrepreneur—a caregiver who would develop a multimillion-dollar business placing other caregivers—worked as much and as long as my mother did. Keesha didn't like being alone, so she would bring her lover in virtually every evening to spend the night with her. While hanging around, I'd be encouraged to color my hair with Jazzing semi-permanent color over the top of my platinum blonde and use the bathroom sink, much to Geraldine's chagrin, as she had the most spotless house. Fortunately, she put up with me destroying her lovely towels. Being at home with Keesha provided a safe haven for me to unwind and be still. We'd known each other since middle school, and no one could communicate with me more effectively than Keesha, who was intensely affectionate, loving, and plain goofy.

It was an art form to lace your car, and it also indicated your come-up for that week. The faster your car became, the more money you made. It was also in the park where everyone obeyed the unwritten rule that no violence of any kind was permitted. It was the only spot and only day where hustlers from all around the city could gather and socialize freely.

The intricacy of the East Coast drug game working in Black neighborhoods from the 1980s to the 1990s has rarely been represented in film or television. The landscape's savagery has been depicted on film, but never its intelligence, inventiveness, and structured nature. I'm no expert, and it's a difficult subject to discuss because there's nothing to brag about. However, it was a truly unique era that has yet to be sufficiently studied to demonstrate why. Furthermore, some of us in the entertainment industry today were educated through that street game. We were taught lessons that allowed us to achieve legitimate achievement and survive in various types of jungles.

My legitimate work also let me connect with all different types of hustlers. They came in to Merry-Go-Round to purchase for themselves and the women in their lives when I worked there. The men who were truly into that life were self-assured, had nothing to prove, held everything close to their chest, and carried a certain quietness that made them a walking secret. Then there were some who were reckless, violent, and unpredictable, and while everyone feared them, their days were always numbered. Arrogance, typical of the boastful, concealed their insecurity—this kind was constantly concerned with themselves and would quickly throw you under the bus. And, believe it or not, many of them had the sweetest hearts hidden underneath the tough shell that protected their wounds.

There were hustlers everywhere. The rink, the clubs, the record store, the apparel stores, my telemarketing job, and a Black family-owned confectionery store in the Harborplace mall. All of these professions and the people I encountered helped me hone my intuition and better understand the inner workings of others.

I wanted to learn everything from Chet from the moment I met him. I appreciated how he conducted himself and his business. He was on the low, low, low, and I knew exactly what was required for success. As he climbed through the ranks, he became my mentor and direct contact, albeit I remained under the protection of BP.

My original ambition of pursuing an acting career became secondary as I began to believe I could become a legitimate queenpin. The timing was perfect. B-more was a drug trafficking hotspot. Our city saw a lot of merchandise travel in and out.

Much of the merchandise was being brought in by traffickers in

Florida, California, and, at times, New York, but New York was hard because of secondhand sales, which reduced earnings. One method of bringing in narcotics was through independent truckers or small truck businesses capable of transporting large-scale supplies. Kilos of cocaine were sometimes packed inside the lining of these vehicles' massive concert-sized speakers. The speakers were disassembled and unloaded after they arrived at a warehouse, and the bricks were ready for distribution. The weights of the shipments ranged from twenty to one hundred kg. The drivers were compensated based on the distance they had to go and the amount of product they were transporting, ranging from $500 to $1,000 per kilo for delivery.

Another method of product concealment was the use of laundry detergent boxes. Before putting the soap powder back into the box, the product has to be vacuum-sealed. Cars were also used and stuffed full of drugs—door panels, engines, inside the seats, spare tires, and even the car's tires. When the car was unloaded, it was a clean, untitled vehicle that could be utilized anyway the receiving party saw fit. Those autos were frequently obtained by side chicks.

More sophisticated techniques for shipping larger quantities of medications evolved throughout time. Legitimate businesses, such as a pool and spa equipment supplier that used hot tubs to deliver cargo, were founded to mask drug shipments. Various firms came up to perform unlawful activities.

This was yet another crash navigation course. Cherry Hill, located in Southwest Baltimore near downtown, was a peninsula surrounded by water that did not function like the rest of the city. There was only one route in and one way out, which was a death trap for my line of work. If you got tangled up on one of the dead-end side streets off the main drag, you could become trapped, kidnapped, and forgotten about. You seldom saw a police car, which made this zone essentially lawless—which had its perks, of course, as I could roll in and out with product and money with little regard for the law. On the other hand, I had to be concerned about the wolves, who were similarly unconcerned by the law.

All of this combined to create a unique and deadly dynamic. But I saw an opening.

For a while, everything went swimmingly. My pockets were fuller than they had ever been. It felt good to be able to share some of my financial freedom with my pals and other women (with whom I might not have been close but who needed assistance to get out of a "sticky" position).

Chet and I enjoyed sharing with individuals in our community in a Robin Hood-like manner, easing hardships where we could. We would sometimes be in the supermarket and see a single mother with children or an elderly person alone and just pay for all of their groceries because we could.

There was so much pain in our environment that we had no idea we were contributing to it.

Pac was working an after-school and weekend job that John had helped him get during this period. He was establishing a vision for his future and blossoming creatively, but as he matured, he became frustrated that he couldn't do more to aid his mother and sister. He felt like he was failing as a man, and he was hard on himself because he felt obligated to provide for those he loved the most.

Pac had never been to Kings Dominion before, so he was delighted to join us. Pac, on the other hand, was always up for a good time. Rodney reached into his pocket as soon as we entered the park to give us money. He certainly had no idea I had my own money. That was probably for the best, because it would have resulted in a very different conversation. Rodney proposed we meet later, at an agreed-upon location, and Pac and I agreed.

We went on rides and ate a lot of junk food, including cotton candy (my favorite), hot dogs, and french fries. We stopped by an installation where you could choose a song by your favorite musician and produce a music video of yourself lip-syncing to it against a green screen.

My thing was, I took any opportunity to perform, and that day I also had the opportunity to have it recorded. Pac was self-conscious since he didn't know all of the lyrics. Because it was previously established that I couldn't rap, I had the easier task. All I had to do was serve as his backup dancer. We argued for a while, but he eventually caved.

And the rest, as they say, is history.

I arrived at school a short time later, without warning—other than the understanding that there were significant conflicts within Pac's home life—and found a letter from him in which Pac delivered the news that he had left for California.

I'd later learn that he'd gone to Donald Hicken days previously to attempt to find a way to stay. Pac kept the entire situation hidden from me. His leave was abrupt, extremely abrupt, and this worried me. Although he assured me in the letter that he was well and would contact me soon, my great concern for his well-being outweighed the reality that he was gone—for good—from Baltimore.

When we eventually spoke, he assured me that he was fine, that he was going from place to place, but that he was safe. He filled me in on the why, but it was tricky. He tried his hardest to make up for his abrupt departure and my desire to make things right for him. I despised the idea that I had no ability to make his life simpler.

I wouldn't allow myself to sense his absence. I needed to keep it moving. I simply kept diving deeper and deeper into the garbage that I thought would get me out of it all.

It's a warm Friday night in late spring 1988, and it all starts with Ramsey and me in a corner booze store on North Ave.

Ramsey is a BSA senior who is soon to graduate. We want to party as much as possible before she leaves for college, so we're going to purchase a bottle of peach schnapps and head down to the port. I have a cheque for $700 from a hair modeling job that I need to cash quickly before I can buy peach schnapps.

I'm standing in line when I notice a tall man in a white T-shirt and pants standing behind me. When the person in front of me exits, I proceed to the bulletproof plexiglass behind which the cashier is hidden. I request schnapps and request that the man pay my check after I sign the back of it. He puts my money underneath the glass toward me, and I grasp it. Just as I'm going to put the money in the top pocket of my jeans jacket, the tall dude behind me grabs my $700 fucking dollars and sprints out the door.

That a joka would reach over me and rob me is the last thing I expect. That's what comes with being short.

I turn around and sprint after the guy, out of the store and down the alley, out of pure instinct and wrath. As I chase him at full speed, I pull my switchblade from my upper jacket pocket, flick it open, and try to catch his ass. All I can think about is how dare you grab my shit! n-gga, not tonight! Tonight is not the night!

We returned to the place, got our peach schnapps, and proceeded down to the waterfront, where we hung out and drank till late at night.

It was a beautiful late-spring night. Evenings like this made me fall in love with the East Coast's warm nights for good. I wanted to savor the pleasure of being outside and hanging out on nights like this for as long as possible. We were having a great time, as we always did when we were together, and I felt like whatever issues were in our way were insignificant.

Then, miraculously... WHO am I looking at? Sure, homeboy! Who stole my shit? Right across the street. The same jeans, sneakers, and white T-shirt. Just mobb'n like nothing ever happened before. But he isn't aware of my presence.

I have to make a decision right now. I stare at him for a few seconds, debating whether I should confront this guy. What I understand is that I don't have the same guts I did in the alley without that flush of adrenaline. Taken note of. I need to quit being so rash—it's going to hurt me.

Turn the other way and leave it alone, I tell myself. I do so while continuing to chuckle with Ramsey.

Despite the preceding events, this night provided me with a lasting impression of my youth's carefreeness. Among all the teachings I was learning at the University of the B-more Streets—Advanced, there was beauty, love, and deep friendship in the midst of everything, with the overt violence and the undertow. And, given the other options and situations that lay ahead for me, this was a very "good" Friday night in a city where you had to be B-more careful since you were now in Murda-land, not Mary-land. Welcome.

Part II: Hollywood

Chapter 5: Living the Dream

"Are we going to the club or what?" I asked my friend MC Lyte one Saturday night.

We met at an awards event for ACT-SO, a New York-based charity that gives scholarships to students in the arts and sciences. I felt like a dream had come true when I discovered Lyte was a member of the program. Talk about one of the most distinct and unusual voices in the game! She was my female rap idol, and she should be thankful I can't rap because I would have tried to take her entire steeze.

I could seriously drink a lot of people under the table and still be on my feet back then. It was the Pinkett inside of me. Lyte was often by my side when I was completely out of control. Despite the fact that she partied hard in her own right, she always had the foresight to make sure I didn't get into too much trouble.

Before we even went out on this Saturday night, I'd downed nearly a full bottle of red wine (her preferred beverage), smoked enough pot to almost pass out, and then taken a tab of X.

I finished it off with a shot of Courvoisier before we left. Brown liquor, in particular, was usually the entryway to my more aggressive, dark side, though I believe it was the combination of various mind-altering substances that got me going that night.

The entire club culture in Los Angeles at the time was insane. As in dreadful. Apart from gay clubs, most well-known clubs didn't have excellent music, and most people were on the dance floor to be seen rather than to dance. However, every now and again, a hot DJ will come through and take over an underground club or restaurant/bar, and word will spread. A lively throng would occasionally show up.

I kept spouting nonsense, laughing, joking, and generally being the noisy mess that I am when I am fucked up.

I had an emptiness inside of me that I couldn't fill but refused to accept. Why would I do that? I was supposed to be happy, and those who accomplish what I did in such a short period of time are supposed to be happy.

On a daily basis, I was reminded of this in a city that promises a happily ever after if you work hard enough.

Even though I was making substantial money—legally, too—at the age of nineteen, nothing was assured, and rather than squander it all on opulent furnishings, vehicles, and jewelry, I kept my life and my new apartment basic and humble. Old habits, such as being on the low, are difficult to break. The rent was cheap for this huge three-bedroom two-story condo, which included a garage and a two-car carport, as well as a wide rear patio and a large garden. There was a lovely stained-glass window above the front door, and the decor was earthy and rustic, with plenty of wood. My favorite feature was not one, but two wood-burning fireplaces—one in the living room and one in my bedroom—a boyhood fantasy come true. I didn't know anyone who had a fireplace in their bedroom, so it meant I'd built it.

There was a family feeling at work. I couldn't have wished for a more encouraging set of folks by my side as I grew into my own. There were two people who were always in my corner: Kadeem Hardison (Dwayne Wayne) and Jasmine Guy (Whitley), both elder siblings watching out for the young wild one. I really met Kadeem through Duane Martin—they were good friends—and we became quick friends. Jas was basically a badass girl—a girl's girl who was attractive, witty, very brilliant, and didn't take crap. That's my kind of lady. Darryl Bell, Karen Malina White, Ajai Sanders, Dawnn Lewis, Glynn Turman, Charnele Brown, Bumper Robinson, Patrick Malone, and Lou Myers all performed admirably as castmates. I was fortunate to be cast in such a talented group for my first television show.

Darryl M. Bell, who played the character Ron on the show, was another activist. Darryl, a super-intelligent man with an elephant's memory, never forgot how I persuaded him to accompany me to Baltimore to speak to Black youngsters about the importance of education and the chances it provides. He was incredibly courteous and generous with his time, connecting his personal entrepreneurial path to the lesson we were delivering. Darryl and I were nominated for an NAACP Image Award for our efforts to empower youth.

I recognized the blinders that come with not being able to view life beyond your own experience when I spoke to kids who reminded me of myself at their age. Education enables you to see that you have dreams that you are unaware of. I became interested in assisting in the creation of educational possibilities for individuals incarcerated after visiting juvenile detention centers and women's prisons in numerous states. My early activities included the construction of libraries in underserved schools in Baltimore and Los Angeles. Growing up, I was no academic standout, but books provided a constant source of comfort.

I had dabbled with devoted relationships, but at this point, I had opted to forego becoming committed. After all, the world was literally my oyster. Why would I give up this state of freedom, exploration, and FUNNNNNNNNNNN in the prime of my life? There were many different flavors and kinds. When it came to males, I made no distinctions.

Besides, I didn't think one guy could have all the attributes I was looking for. So I used my Frankenstein method to create a composite image of my ideal man. One guy would be the Intellect and would discuss great concepts. Another example was the Artist, who was in touch with his emotions. I was entertained by the Funny Guy. Then there was the Roughneck Bad Boy—you had to have one of those.

There was also the In the Bed Guy, who was always promised to provide satisfaction. While most of my connections with the other males were platonic, I preferred spending time with them over the In the Bed Guy, who was solely for late-night calls.

When it became evident that I wasn't interested in committing, something unusual happened: the guys who were ordinarily fine with a no-strings-attached arrangement felt compelled to tie me down. Because of my immaturity, I assumed that most males would be relieved by the no-strings-attached get-down. We could simply "enjoy" each other and keep the conversation going. That was very rarely the case. This was a minor revelation about the myth that guys don't feel and have no need for connection. I discovered that the "players" needed connection the most and were simply afraid of yielding to emotional closeness. Exactly like me.

Sex was a distraction for me from having to face my actual need to be held, connected, and loved. It whet the small girl's hunger, who hadn't received enough parental warmth and attention. That dance quickly became irresistible. The sense of entitlement that I should always feel wonderful was a set-up because it could never be satisfied. Gimme, gimme, more, more makes you greedy and confuses what you truly desire.

We normally discuss about exterior addictions like drugs and alcohol, but rarely address interior heart addictions. These are frequently misinterpreted as love, adoration, and connection. Often, it's only lust, which might feed the illusion that you're living your happily ever after.

There have always been stories about me being gay and like ladies. Maybe it had something to do with the clubs where I went, like the Catch, one of the top LGBTQ + venues in L.A. at the time that featured nights for getting up and doing lip-synchs, and where I personally stepped up onstage and lip-synched to all types of music on multiple times. One night, I murdered Madonna's "Vogue" there.

The reality is that during my early years of discovery in Hollywood, I had a few sexual experiences with women, only to discover that I prefer guys when it came to sex. Still, I admire women's beauty on the inside and exterior. And I've never stopped admiring and admiring women of all ages, sizes, and colors. Women, in my opinion, are the most amazing animals on the planet, and I admire them via my friendships.

This period in my life taught me that every woman has the right and the freedom to explore and enjoy her sexuality unapologetically according to her own definition. Unfortunately, many have not. In the years to come, I'd be surprised at how many adult women I knew who'd never had orgasms.

This "let's just have fun" phase with guys was unfortunately brief. I enjoyed the adrenaline rush, but it was only a short high. The intoxicating chase eventually got to me. Now, I've never considered myself an addict of any kind—but that's just denial at work.

Fame may bring you company, but not always good company. And it's absolutely not genuine affection or respect.

As a result, misogyny and objectification of women in rap were complicated what we all actually desired—to be respected, loved, and to feel worthwhile.

I must say that I was impressed. We started talking about making a difference in the neighborhood and helping the youth, and a dope friendship was established. Eazy's true love and emphasis was teaching young people about business and entrepreneurship. He taught me a lot about the value of intellectual property ownership. That was the main shift he cared about: artists owning their work, no matter what it was.

In fact, when I gave him a folder containing some of my poetry (together with artwork by my ex-boyfriend John), Eazy had an entrepreneurial idea. "Publish your poetry and record it as spoken word to music," he said, complimenting me. Along with the book, sell the CD. Own it. "It's all of it."

It was the early 1990s, and nearly no one did anything like this. He was decades ahead of his time. He was a one-of-a-kind character. When he came by and I wasn't home, he'd leave a letter written backwards that you could only read in the mirror. When he paged me, he'd arrange the numbers in such a way that they formed words. His dry sense of humour was unrivaled, yet he could also be extremely stupid.

Eazy usually appeared to have a gray cloud over his head, as if he was overcome with grief. In my naiveté, I couldn't see how tremendous achievement may come with substantial, intricate problems and didn't always imply a happily ever after.

There's a proverb that goes, "We ain't in Kansas no mo." Or something along those lines.

When I went home to Baltimore (aka Kansas) to visit, I knew this was true. I felt weird at a place that was previously so familiar to me. Not any longer. People, understandably, found it difficult to comprehend the reality I was living. They, like me, believed that fame and wealth would cure all woes. Surprise—I had changed, but my problems had not.

It would take me many years to understand the distinction between having confidence in certain aspects of my life (performing, making money, and living in survival mode) and having a healthy sense of self-worth. Confidence can aid in the development of self-worth, but it cannot replace self-love.

When you don't know this, you're constantly trying to prove yourself.

You convince yourself, If I only acquire a little more success and learn how to do it well, I can... all those things that, if we obtain more, if we repair our imperfections, appear cuter, lose weight, get a nose job, buy a new car, start a new relationship, or a few of them, we will be fine.

If I dared to confess that I was still looking for and fighting to achieve real happiness among the flash and glamour of Hollywood, it came off as ungrateful and spoiled. I couldn't tell if something was wrong with me or if I was just being ungrateful. It was perplexing.

At home, I was looking forward to being Jada without having to be on. That didn't always happen, but returning home provided a chance to reset and reconnect with loved ones. Many loved ones, understandably, wanted to be near Hollywood when I was in town.

When I returned to Baltimore, I went to see my grandma Shirley and was astonished that she had organized an autograph session without informing me. When I arrived, the first thing I noticed was people on the porch outside, followed by folks in the living room and kitchen waiting for me inside. What I had really been looking forward to was sitting down in her kitchen and playing Boggle as I used to as a youngster.

Shirley had done nothing wrong. She was overjoyed to give everyone an opportunity to see me. I went along with it, took the pictures, and signed the autographs, but I wasn't happy about it.

Shirley exclaimed, "What's wrong with you?" as everyone began to depart.

"I wasn't expecting all of these people here," I said, hoping that was the end of it. How do you explain to your grandma that you don't want to be celebrated by her and her friends when that's all she wants? That seemed ludicrous even to me. But that's how I felt.

My explanation was not well received.

I turned twenty in the fall of 1991. Birthdays had always been significant to me, and Pac was there to help me celebrate.

Pac has also recently made his cinematic acting debut in Juice. Ernest R. Dickerson's directing debut, as well as his acting, drew a lot of notice in Hollywood. Pac was flying high, yet despite his achievement, he felt the same void I did. Fortunately, we could confide in one another.

We shared many of the same concerns and frustrations, but his were greater in scope and his life was more difficult than mine. Pac had a lot of responsibilities and had to look after a lot of people while also trying to figure out how to look after himself. He also had to deal with the strains of hip-hop street politics and simply being a young Black man in America with recognition. This put a new type of bullseye on his back that he hadn't seen coming.

None of this was going the way we expected it to. The fact that we had each other as tethers was a saving grace.

When I had some money and Pac didn't, I used to be the one keeping an eye on things. And when he had some money and I didn't, he kept an eye on me—like when I was in college. We were now on parallel rails. It was bizarre, even inconceivable, that we would both be on such a high at the same time.

Sharing the rising was the most lovely and unexpected part of the dream, as flawed as it was at times. We had each other to lean on when we were stumbling, trying to figure out how to manage the new influx of money and status that is always accompanied by higher expenses, increased pressure to take on the financial responsibilities of our immediate and extended families and friends, and every other demand of being the "it" commodity. Nobody prepares you, especially when you're nineteen or twenty and don't know who to trust.

Pac seemed to keep me from seeing him in his new orbit at times. I spent very little time in his company. This was something new. When I offered that I go see him perform, he flatly refused. He'd turn up no matter where I was. But he sought to keep me apart from his world and everything that went with it. Unexpected shit was always bouncing off him, which he couldn't always handle. In retrospect, I can understand that he wanted to keep me safe.

As a result, I never saw Pac perform live. Of course, this was only meant to be a temporary solution. But we were always on the lookout for new ways to interact creatively. That was a must for both of us.

He couldn't stop talking about the project. He was ecstatic about the prospect and went on to remark that the young directors, twins named Hughes, were quite skilled. He was certain that they were going to make a good picture, and that it would be more raw than Boyz n the Hood.

A scenario like this is quite rare in Hollywood. It was difficult for an actress to transition from a TV sitcom to a gritty feature film back then. (These days, it's much less of a problem for performers to work in both television and film.) Besides, I was under contract with NBC and wasn't really accessible at the time. Plus, as Pac reminded me, I had to audition for the film.

"Naw," he insisted, "I told the directors you're my homegirl." They only need to meet you. I told them you were ideal for the part."

Who knew my first Hollywood film would be starring with Pac in a role he cast me in?

Pac arranged for me to meet directors Allen and Albert Hughes. We all liked each other when we first met. They liked my audition for the part of Ronnie, a single mother. And it appeared that the deal was done in an instant.

Not exactly.

When the offer came in, I went to see Debbie Allen to inform her about the film, and she was so delighted for me that she channeled her magic into convincing the network and producers to let me do the film while finishing out the final season of A Different World. Debbie was not going to let me pass up such an opportunity. On her watch, no way. "Don't be concerned, bunny rabbit. We'll figure something out. My child will star in her own film." Debbie completed the task as promised.

I felt prepared and ready now that I had overcome the most difficult obstacle.

THEN, shortly after the transaction was completed, Pac called me upstairs in my bedroom. He'd gotten into a fight with the Hughes brothers.

I sat on the side of my bed, motionless, staring at the phone as if it were to blame. The dream of the two of us working together in my debut film was dashed. I only wanted to make Menace II Society because of him.

I didn't even bother returning his call. He was fortunate because I couldn't contact Debbie Allen and tell her, "I'm sorry, after all you did to fight for me, I don't want to do this movie now."

What the fuck?! was all I could think as I laid back and looked up at the canopy.

When all was said and done, I had to give Pac credit. He possessed what I would call sight, which I did not yet have. Menace II Society aided in the serious, rapid-fire launch of my cinematic career, even leading to the Cannes cinematic Festival, one of the world's most famous film festivals. That doesn't happen very often for Black

Baltimore actresses. Just a thought. Pac had that vision, not mine.

The trip to the French Riviera in southern France was considered a rite of passage. Nobody had actually prepared me for strolling the red carpet before our film's screening. Nobody ever mentioned hiring a stylist to help them choose an outfit and dress for the foreign press. I had no idea. What I believed was an avant-garde, daring ensemble turned out to be me dressed as Bozo the Clown, in slacks and a long orange top with yellow and orange circles that resembled polka dots. Not my greatest appearance.

Working on the first significant project with the Hughes brothers was, for the most part, a liberating experience. They allowed me a lot of latitude to act out a scenario the way my gut told me I should, based on my personal experiences. The film was a critical and commercial triumph. It was a blessing in every way to be a part of it.

I'd use any opportunity to thank him for his contribution to the beginning of my film career, even if he didn't think he deserved it. "You looked out for me when you didn't have to," he would say more than once. That is why I will always adore you with all my heart. Always."

He was always present in my life. He was always there when I called. Whatever the case may be.

Chapter 6: Breakdown

When Duane Martin stated that his good buddy Will Smith wanted to fly in to chat to me about a role while we were filming The Inkwell in Wilmington, North Carolina, I thought, "Cool."

I had some spare time. For God's sake, I was in Wilmington.

"He's flying in tomorrow."

We didn't have many options for places to visit. We were sleeping in the opulent suites of the Holiday Inn on the outskirts of Wilmington. Next door was Hooters, where women in tight T-shirts served pitchers of beer and plates of hot wings. Our only other option was a shabby, darkly lit Chinese restaurant with a Southern tinge, which felt so out of place.

Will came to North Carolina from Atlanta, Georgia, where he was working on a project, and we met at the Chinese restaurant. Will began by claiming that he'd traveled down to personally ask me if I'd play his series regular girlfriend on The Fresh Prince of Bel-Air. The show had been a big success for several seasons, so the decision seemed obvious. The show was successful. But I wasn't interested in returning to television at the moment.

Since Menace, I've had a slew of film chances come my way. "Thank you for flying all the way here, but I don't want to do TV right now," I explained to Will as politely as I could. Thank you for the chance." That was the end of it.

Will was courteous and understanding, and he departed as quickly as he arrived.

Duane began harassing me at the restaurant and then accompanied me to my suite at the Holiday Inn—not fancy but spacious—to persuade me to reconsider. His worry was that Hollywood was not consistently producing lead roles for Black actresses. On a crossover megahit comedy series like Fresh Prince, he also emphasized the necessity of a guaranteed paycheck. He pointed out that it didn't have to derail my cinematic career. "You can do both TV and movies, you know," he went on to say.

I concurred. Only—"That's not what I want to do." Despite the odds, I wanted to try my hand at being a movie star, even though I had nothing planned for the future. That was a gamble. By the same token, what if I returned to TV and lost my hard-earned position as a film actress?

I was confident in my decision both then and now. When you didn't always have a Debbie Allen to battle for you to do movies, movies allowed me the option to perform a range of parts, go from project to project, and not be stuck in one role on TV, under contract.

I was introduced to Doug and George after a total makeover. Doug and George finally gave me the thumbs up after that, and with poor Allen Payne pleading like crazy for how ideal he thought I was for the role. This film, thanks to Maxine and Judy, was a watershed moment for me, allowing me to soften those edges.

Jason's Lyric was the first film I'd made with an explicit love scene, which I didn't want to do. The producers had agreed in advance to hire a body double, but they had a difficult time locating someone who looked like me. Later, I encountered the same problem with Set It Off and didn't notice the mismatch until the screening. Although the body double's juicy bottom was quite enticing, it was not my less juicy booty.

I like making movies, but the daily whiplash of doubting my worth got to me. Babyyyyy, I would be continually reminded, more than ever, of how inadequate I was—while also being lauded. It was perplexing for a twenty-year-old like me. It seemed like I was on a hamster wheel, a merry-go-round, chasing a carrot: Your performance is stunning. And now for the Jason's Lyric poster: Is your thigh visible? We're sorry, but it's too provocative, so we're removing your thigh.

I was sick of getting kissed on one cheek and then backhanded on the other. It was one thing to strive for self-improvement and to meet the expectations of a leading lady, but where did it end? How could you play the game without becoming too engrossed? To the point where you let the game entirely identify you?

I had no choice except to swallow my misery, as I was accustomed to doing. It was a dash for the flowers to avoid any nagging anxieties or dissatisfaction. They'd just slow you down.

Earthquakes are extremely difficult to forecast. There are times when you feel tremors ahead of time, but this is not a norm. They frequently strike without warning. This is the best way I can characterize an otherwise routine day as I drive down Melrose Avenue. A girlfriend sees me driving by in her car and flags me down. I turn around in the middle of the street to follow her automobile to the curb. I step out, and we exchange greetings.

I hop back into my car and drive away, but after a few moments, I realize I'm too shaken to drive.

I turned onto a side street, parked, and tried to pull myself together through torrential tears and an avalanche of emotions as I approached the next corner. My heart was thumping out of my chest, my breath was short, and I couldn't fight off a tidal wave of sadness—a sorrow that was about to drown me if I didn't get control of myself. Fear and unrelenting grief had sucka-punched me.

When I returned home to an empty house, my despair gave way to an impulse I'd never had before: that this pain within had to stop, that it was so awful that the only alternative was to stop life. The more I tried to forget about slashing my wrist, the more terrified I got that I might actually do it. For the first time in my life, I didn't rely solely on myself.

Lyte truly carried her light into my gloom once she arrived, never leaving my side for a single minute of the day and never asking questions. She was great company, keeping me grounded and distracting me from feeling out of control. She, like my dogs, normalized my days because she was never one for drama. Routine can be calming. We'd get up, head to Vivian's, my favorite breakfast location, and then hang out with the Rotts. Lyte was more than an anchor in a stormy sea, a symbol that everything would be fine till my mother swooped in.

My seams broke all over again when my mother arrived. Mom had only been sober for a year at the time, and she only had two weeks to stay, during which she did everything she could to console and assist me. She was in touch with how our history could effect me after working her steps in recovery.

She then proposed that we go to therapy together. The thought of unlocking the full Pandora's box with my mother was too much for me at the time.

But I was aware that I required assistance. That caused me to contact Debbie Allen, a phone call that began, "I'm not doing well... I need some assistance, someone to talk to..."

Debbie, as always, acted quickly and arranged for me to be seen the following day by Dr. Sally Grieg, the nicest therapist who, without a doubt, saved my life. She requested that I consult a psychiatrist after my first session with her so that I may be prescribed some medication.

She had a warm, maternal demeanor, and I trusted and felt her genuineness. I gave up my fight when we promised that after I'd stabilized, I'd get off the Prozac as soon as possible.

The procedure took longer than anticipated. When I first started taking the drug, I was disappointed that it had eliminated my libido. That was not going to work for me for a long time. Sex was the only good thing in my life. However, as Dr. Grieg predicted, the medicines assisted me in getting my head above the dark clouds, and therapy assisted me in beginning a road of emotional healing. At the very least, I could recognize where the wounds came from and then begin the difficult work of forgiveness and acceptance.

In the early stages of my recuperation, I was ready to leave Hollywood and purchased a farmhouse outside of Baltimore. It needed a lot of work, but the idea was for me to return home. This way, I could go to Los Angeles or New York for auditions, but I no longer wanted to be a part of the Hollywood scene.

I needed some quiet time. I needed some peace and quiet. I needed to take a deep breath.

Chapter 7: Trying to Find My Footing

The main draw of the farmhouse I bought on the outskirts of Baltimore was its old-world elegance, with a beautiful hearth in the kitchen and a small pond off the terrace, all on a wide plot of land. The views from the farmhouse windows were stunning, and I was confident they would be in every season. I intended to fill my new home with a collection of rescued dogs and kittens, possibly even a horse for my mother, fulfilling a childhood dream of hers.

I meant to move into the farmhouse as my primary residence, but that couldn't happen immediately soon, so I stayed in L.A. while monitoring the repairs, making short, frequent visits.

When I returned to the East Coast, being close to family helped me regain my bearings and feel grounded. Surprisingly, life in Baltimore felt a little simpler and slower than it used to. When I stayed with my mother, who was now totally committed to her recovery and living in Columbia, Maryland, in a new, stable relationship with Paul Jones (soon to be her third husband), I had a sense of security that I hadn't felt in a long time, if ever.

The fact that Adrienne lived in the suburbs helped to alleviate my rising fear of being kidnapped and imprisoned for ransom. Part of this was due to PTSD from the violence I had already experienced. Part of it was the realization that abduction was becoming a new business in Baltimore, and that now that I was a well-known rising celebrity, people would assume I was a lucrative target. I walked more cautiously since I didn't want to end up duct-taped in a car trunk. And, sadly, I knew people who had been victimized... and those who were perpetrators. My response was to be extra cautious.

That was a good concept, and we all agreed on it.

The four of us were soon up on Ventura Boulevard at Jerry's, a popular hangout that stayed open late. Will was not the ridiculous character I had suspected him to be. He was a great communicator, extremely intelligent, well-read, and infectiously passionate about a wide range of topics. He progressed from Plato to Z-3 MCs (old-school hip-hop) to politics and eventually took over the table with his dramatic narration. He was also amusing and seemed to have a level of stability that was refreshing. He had a broad vision, not just for his work, but he made no apologies for his desire to become the world's largest movie star and to seize all that life had to offer.

Professionally, I didn't miss a beat. The survivor in me understood better than to disclose my problems in order to avoid being labeled "unreliable" for job. In 1994, I was on a merry-go-round, either handling PR for a batch of films released that year, shooting other projects, or putting in hours for another batch in pre- or post-production.

I could be in Washington, D.C., one night for the premiere of A Low Down Dirty Shame (which was memorable because I invited Robsol and he showed up in a red leather suit, as esoteric and stylish as ever), and flying back to L.A. the next day for fittings on Demon Knight, directed by Ernest Dickerson and executive-produced by Joel Silver as part of Tales from the Crypt.

It was my good fortune, I thought, to avoid being typecast and to delve deeply into character development and motivation in both drama and comedy. I got the opportunity to train with a fight teacher for my character as Peaches during pre-production for A Low Down Dirty Shame—to make it plausible that I could physically kick a grown man's ass.

Getting behind the camera—and coming up with the video concept—proved to me that my creativity was not restricted to being in front of the camera. I suddenly found myself balancing acting and directing, so I had to be mindful of how I used my time, both professionally and socially. However, the two did occasionally collide.

The meeting was scheduled within days—at my house—and I was still in shock when I opened the door. He was dressed all in white and smiling warmly as I welcomed him into my living room and pulled out my photo albums to illustrate that I was a true fan!

I had no idea Prince would be humiliated by my actions because I was so eager to show him those images. Needless to say, he was horrified (there was no resemblance), which made me adore him even more.

What began as his interest in potentially cooperating on some project ideas quickly evolved into a lovely, long-lasting friendship, as well as his kindness to me as a mentor. While he was assisting me in finding my feet, Prince was also attempting to find his in his battle with his label, Warner Bros. Records, for artistic liberty. He was unwavering in his message to fellow creatives about not enabling the industry to benefit from your creativity. His desire to reclaim the masters to his music, to own both his art and his name, was a recurring issue throughout our meetings.

I loved his tenacity, how powerfully expressive he was, and what he was ready to risk in order to challenge the powers that be. In contrast to his dandy-esque tendencies, Prince loved to have fun and had a wicked sense of humour, as well as a dash of "hood magic."

One of the first musicians I saw take over an entire cinema screen was Prince. We entered through the back door, and I must have been pressing my point about something as we walked along.

When he appeared out of nowhere to befriend me, I was reassured by his kindness, respect, and appreciation for my talent. He provided me with knowledge, insight, and support that I really needed at the moment.

Although I wasn't ready for a meaningful commitment, by the fall of 1994, I was ready to call it quits on boys. Then I received an intriguing phone call. Publicists and managers were frequently used to make Hollywood introductions during this time period. That's how I consented to go on a date with a gentleman named Lance. I granted the request because... well, why not?

Lance appeared intent on tying me down from our first meeting. He arrived bearing gifts, trips, and accolades galore, as well as a declaration of his desire to have a child with me. This guy didn't know who I was, and even though I told him I wasn't interested in a committed relationship, he persisted. He wasn't hearing me, to the point where he requested me to meet his other child.

"It's too soon, and we really don't know where this is going," I kindly told him. We should hold off on that."

Then, assuming I'd bite, he went all out and offered to pay over $700,000 toward the refurbishment of my farmhouse in Maryland. Yes, it was an expensive position, and it was tempting, but I'd learned a long time ago that nothing comes for free. His gesture didn't feel generous; it felt like a ruse to trap me. When I denied his present and he became enraged, my mother yanked me up and said, "I don't like him, Jada. "There's something strange about him."

I thought my mother's concern was excessive, and as naive young daughters do, I dismissed her reaction. But I had a nagging sensation within that Mommie was correct. He had displayed indicators of being easily upset and having problems settling down when he did not get his way. Because I was young, I reasoned, "Why not give the dude a chance in case I'm missing something?" There was a tenderness to him, and I have to say, all that attention made me feel desirable again, especially after my collapse. So I rationalized, "Perhaps he's just an extremely generous person who is excited about the prospect of us as a couple."

Lance lived out of state, and I'd visited him a few times and had a good time. As a result, when Lance invited me to travel back with him to his house shortly after Thanksgiving, I accepted, telling him, "I can't stay long."

I had only been at Lance's for two days when I received a series of calls in the early morning of November 30 telling me that I needed to travel for New York.

Pac was ambushed and shot outside Quad Recording Studios near Times Square around 12:35 a.m. that day. He'd been wounded five times and was brought to Bellevue for treatment of his most serious wound, a gunshot to the groin. The updates I received from Pac's mother, Afeni, were optimistic. Pac had survived, and we no longer had to wonder whether he would live or die.

Pac, on the other hand, was due in court the next day—December 1—in an ongoing sexual assault case arising from an event in November 1993. Pac had first sought to explain the grounds for the claim to me while I was visiting him in New York. We were in his hotel room, discussing his new Interscope Records project, Me Against the World. I was ecstatic about the CD and glad for him. Pac then looked at me with true earnestness as the subject went to his latest legal issues and stated, "I need to explain to you what happened." "How I got this case."

I braced myself for a ferocious rebuttal, not because he disagreed with that notion, but because you never knew which Pac would show up on any given day. Depending on his mood and whether he gave a fuck about your viewpoint, he might be confrontational. On this particular time, however, he sat silently across from me in a chair. Something was moving in Pac. His vitality was infused with more humility and openness than I had witnessed in a minute. We sat there in silence for a long time, and I remember thinking that once everything was finished, he would act completely differently. His world had gone out of hand, and he had become disoriented. I regarded this as a wake-up call for him.

Pac maintained throughout the legal procedures that he did not commit the alleged abuse but accepted responsibility for not stopping those who did.

Layers of misunderstanding about my relationship with Pac had tormented me in my romantic relationships. So I could be patient with Lance's discomfort, but the way he reacted didn't win me over. "That n-gga just so happens to be one of my best friends," I explained, calm yet flustered.

Even though I knew Pac had been released from Bellevue, the looming issues were WHO had ambushed him, WHY, and HOW I might help arrange for his safety. The first order of business was to get Pac through his court date and then to a secret location where he could rest. I didn't have time for Lance's fears.

It was weird to travel to New York. Pac was waiting for his hearing in a dirty hallway, accompanied by Afeni and several other individuals, when I arrived at the courthouse. I'll never forget seeing Tupac after the attack, bandaged up and in a wheelchair. I'd never seen him that vulnerable before. There was nothing I could say or do to make things better. He was in anguish, coping with an intense court case, a serious assassination attempt, and the media circus. I just wanted to hug him, but I couldn't.

Everything was in disarray, and he was convinced that someone was out to murder him. Pac was invited to come out and stay at my house, but Afeni and I reasoned that if someone was looking for him, my house would be a top choice for where to look.

It was agreed that I should keep my distance until we knew what was going on.

But it was difficult to be distracted because I was always in communication with Jasmine and Pac. That must have gnawed at Lance.

A couple of days passed. Nothing huge occurred, but I did receive another very critical phone call. I just didn't realize how important it was at the time. Spike Lee had contacted me about a script he was working on called Girl 6. Spike called and discussed the project, concluding, "I'll send you the script, see what you think, and then we should meet."

I was pleased to be on Spike's radar, even though I didn't think that particular project was suited for me. When I later told Lance about the call, he was uninterested.

Lance brought me and a friend out to supper the next night. Everything appeared to be very peaceful and consistent. On our way home, I remember glancing out the window and noticing landmarks that had grown familiar by this point. I had adopted this practice anytime I was in a new area because of my new dread of being kidnapped and the necessity to have an escape plan on hand.

We were only three minutes away from Lance's house when a little disagreement between us escalated into an emotional outburst from him. His intensity never felt safe, so my usual reaction was to attempt to remain calm.

My pulse thumped, and I quickly examined the surroundings outside the car, determining where we were and how far we were from his house. Lance slammed on the brakes and turned to strike me as I made my assessment. I threw open the car door and ran across the street in my flat sandals and skirt, going through some backyards to get to the house before he did.

I knew he kept his back sliding door open, so I dashed into the house from his backyard, veered into the bedroom, where I quickly grabbed my black Russell sweatpants and sneakers, and then raced into the kitchen, where I grabbed the biggest knife he had before hiding in his child's empty bedroom.

I consider my alternatives as I change into my sweatpants. It's late, I don't know anyone in the area, and there's no way I can leave securely. I've got until the morning to get on the first plane out of here. Lance's voice echoes through the house as he walks through the sliding back door, before I can finish tying my sneakers: "JADA! WHERE IN THE WORLD ARE YOU?"

He keeps yelling for me as I realize—FUCK!—I'm trapped in a small room with only walls surrounding me. There are no doors or windows. Trapped. I'm done if he finds me, as enormous and pumped as he is. Even with a knife, I have no escape or advantage. I feel panic rising within me, but instead of succumbing to it, I find enough anger within myself to move.

I decide to try to shoot for the front door. Lance emerges from his bedroom at the far end of the corridor opposite me the moment I step into it. We're at a stalemate. Lance is walking quickly toward me until I draw the massive knife and hold it out in front of me.

My heart rate slows. I know neither of us will come out of this undamaged. He starts creeping closer me, as if trying to convince me that I'm secure, which I know isn't the case.

Thankfully, Lance's friend enters the house through the front door and immediately attempts to deescalate the situation. Lance's friend calms things down sufficiently for him to apologize for how far things have gotten.

I answer quickly by playing along, accepting his apology, and agreeing, "Of course." I see what you're saying. I'm sure you didn't intend it. Everything is in order." And so forth.

As soon as everything seemed to be going well, I surreptitiously called my assistant and requested her to get me on a plane to Los Angeles the next morning.

Lance noticed me packed and inquired, "Where are you going?"

"Remember when I told you about my phone call with Spike?" He wants to meet with me in L.A. tomorrow, but I'll return later."

Lance was aware of what was going on but let it go for the night, mainly because I'd mentioned Spike earlier. When the car arrived the next morning to haul me up, Lance replied, "I'm never going to see you again, am I?"

"Of course you will," I answered with my best, most forgiving smile. I'll call you after I finish my meeting."

I boarded the plane, holding my breath, grateful that the lie had worked. I never saw Lance again—not alone.

We were in constant contact from the minute Pac arrived at Rikers, whether on the phone or through a flood of letters, and he didn't hold back in giving me the lowdown. One of the first letters, sent at two a.m., described how he spent his days striving to drain the guards' "shouts of power" and ignoring the "diabolical laughs" of "hollow men happy to be incarcerated." He compared himself to a bird without wings unable to fly to freedom and a fish "far from the sea" unable to breathe.

I would try to be home at specific times to receive his phone calls. My schedule was demanding, but we found a way to communicate frequently. We were still hoping that his appeal would result in a stay of execution and that he would not have to serve his sentence. He was considering anything from two to seven years. The legal expenses were piling up, and I took care of a few of them to keep the ship afloat. Fortunately, he did not object, but I proceeded with caution.

Then, on February 2/3, I received a letter from Pac that completely caught me off guard. It was addressed to "JK Shakur" (Jada Koren, Pac's surname).

I slowly opened the mail and read the note. Pac began by admitting that he was aware that we had not been romantic in the past, but that he had arrived at the conclusion that the two of us were meant to be husband and wife. He stated that when he was struggling, people claimed to love him, but "only you loved me," and that when he blew up, "everybody swore they loved me," but only I did, in his opinion. And he went on to say, "Now that I've fallen from grace and the world has turned against me, a few claim to love me, but you show me your love once more." After much introspection and spiritual awareness, I realized that the friend, lover, and soulmate was always present. I have never witnessed or felt the intensity and loyalty that you have shown me.

Pac contacted my mother and formally requested my hand in marriage. Pac was a traditionalist, especially when it came to certain conventional ideals. He was a firm believer in family and loyalty, and he adored children. I had never seen myself getting married, and I had no intention of ever doing so. To whoever. Nonetheless, one thing I knew about Pac was that he would eventually marry and become a devoted father.

Mommie adored Pac, but she did not believe we should marry. She advised Pac that if this was what we truly desired, we should wait to see how things went with his case before making any commitments. When I mentioned Pac's marriage proposal to Afeni, she was very diplomatic: "I want you guys to do what makes you happy."

Everyone was surprised by what had happened, but none of them had seen Pac at Rikers. I had, and I knew exactly how Pac felt. Still, I couldn't shake the feeling that the two of us as husband and wife would be a disaster.

I experimented with the possibility throughout my uncertainties. Until I asked Pac, "Do you expect me to come there for conjugal visits?"

Yes, he replied. This is when reality kicked in. Pac expected me to be more than simply a psychological wife, but also a physical wife. It was impossible for me. Pac and I eventually reached a point of acceptance after several long chats.

Pac wanted me as a wife to get him through his prison sentence, but not for the rest of his life. He didn't realize it at the time, not while he was in jail, but once he was out, he was pleased he didn't marry me.

Pac was convicted in court on February 8 to serve between eighteen months and four and a half years. According to the New York Times, he tearfully apologized to his victim while claiming that he was not guilty of the crime. Pac was transported upstate to the maximum-security jail in Dannemora, New York, around Valentine's Day 1995.

We couldn't believe it. Dannemora, in Tupac's words, was "where they send you if you kill someone or blow up the World Trade Center." Terrorists had attempted to blow up the World Trade Center two years earlier, only to return to do the job in 2001. What happened to the terrorists? Dannemora.

Pac was in that location.

Chapter 8: The Reluctant Bride

Will's grandma Gigi learned from Will's sister Ellen that her grandson was dating someone new during the early stages of our courtship, which we were keeping hidden.

"Oh, so we keep'n secrets from each other now, loverboy?" Gigi remarked as she took up the phone. Or something along those lines.

Will told his grandmother that he wasn't hiding anything, that he and I were dating, and that we'd all meet soon. Will had arranged for Gigi to travel out to California within days so that proper introductions could be made.

Will decided to have Gigi watch Jason's Lyric before I got at his place at the scheduled time. Which, by the way, includes a very naked sex scene in the woods (in which I had a body double because I refused to do nudity). Consider this: I'm meeting my new boyfriend's grandmother for the first time, and when I walk in, she's sitting on the couch, arms folded, shaking her head. She continues, "I don't know why young people feel like they gotta take their clothes off to make movies."

I grin, hug her, and motion for Will to join me in the rear bedroom as I say to his grandmother, "Excuse us a minute, Gigi." I couldn't believe he'd performed such a trick on me, and I was furious: "Why would you EVER do that to me?" "What on earth are you thinking?"

"I promise you, Babe. This will be amusing later."

"It's not humorous. That lady is your granny. "Can you see how she's staring at me?"

With that, I summoned all of my diplomatic skills—along with some acting—and returned to Gigi, laughing like it was nothing.

Will and I are still discussing whether or not that was humorous.

However, it was a bonding event for Gigi and myself. I didn't have to put on any airs after that. I was free to be myself since I had nothing to hide. Literally. For the record, I eventually brought up the nude scene, telling her, "Gigi, you know, that wasn't actually me on the screen," to which she simply smiled at me and tenderly shooed me away with her hand.

We traveled frequently to see Will's family in Philadelphia and my family in Baltimore. Growing up surrounded by matriarchs in my own family made it easy to get to know the matriarchs in Will's life. Miss Carolyn, called Mom-Mom, Will's mother, had a special place in my heart. She was genuine, substantial, and powerful. I loved her elegance in light of her life experiences, and how, despite a difficult marriage to Will Sr., as Daddio, and a subsequent divorce, she supported Will's desire to have both parents present for significant events and holiday celebrations. She was an educator and school board member who was also an activist. Mom-Mom was always a lovely example of what faith, strength, and patience might bring to this human experience.

Regarding my mother and Will, she went from urging me not to talk to him since he was married at the time (a wise decision) and advising us not to date (because he was divorced with a child and it would be complicated) to now pronouncing him the most lovely guy on the earth. Will had her in fits of laughter all of a sudden. He couldn't possibly go wrong. She adored him, and when it came to having fun, they were a match made in heaven.

It was a blessing in so many ways that our families embraced our relationship and each other. Families do not always get along, and because family was essential to us both, this was a shared fundamental value that provided us with a stable foundation that should not be taken for granted.

We were getting ready to go out one evening when I got out of the shower and Will discovered that I had missed quite a few bikini-waxing appointments. To be honest, I had given up on going. "You see, you're a guy, so you don't understand the pain of it all." I could go on and on. Will was searching through my closet as I was making my case. He discovered my black knit cap with short black dreads all over it.

I had sat on the bed to apply lotion to my feet when I noticed Will standing up. He stood there in his briefs, raised up into a Brazilian-bikini fit, my hat's curling dreads sprouting out like unkempt pubic hair on all sides in a forest-sized bush.

That was plainly his forte. And it was both disarming and infuriating to be upset at him because he could always manage to crack a joke. I would refuse to laugh at times, hoping that he would realize he had chosen an improper time to try to be amusing. This would be a futile endeavor.

Humor was an elixir he could pour. He utilized his intellect concoction to similar effect. A tango based on a common love of learning led to intense intellectual banter as part of our seductive dance. We could go toe-to-toe from sunrise to sunset, arguing and debating about anything. We'd end up reading the same book in order to start the great disputes. We loved keeping each other guessing, whether it was The Tao of Physics or A History of God. Will is the only person on the earth who can provide my thoughts with greater conversation. We can and do converse for hours on end.

First and foremost, we developed a friendship that served as the foundation of our partnership. But no relationship is flawless, and the pace of our life didn't allow for a conventional honeymoon phase. We were also embarking on a large life, and neither of us had the emotional maturity to deal with it. However, the difficulties produced a link that existed outside of romance because things became too real too quickly and we had to figure out how to handle them together. In some ways, my desire for Will to be my Savior Prince was romantic. For both of us, it was a classic setup.

Cesar and I met on a regular basis, and he'd bring his pack, which included his assistant teacher, Daddy, the most amazing pit bull I'd ever encountered, in addition to my daily routine with the dogs. We'd then plan a serious hike as a group.

As I discovered, divorce is rarely amicable. It's brutal, no matter how much two people want to avoid it. Will internalized a lot of what was happening to him. To his credit, he did his best to be a caring presence for his son, Trey, who was a baby when his parents divorced.

Trey was a clever, lively, and confident child with an alluring sweetness. My priority the first time I got to spend a day with Trey was to plan an exciting, memorable adventure. Where should I go? I pondered and pondered. Then it dawned on me: a candy store!

What child doesn't like candy? It wasn't just any old store. It was like Halloween on steroids in this sweet utopia, with every classic and new candy ever manufactured. Trey's eyes were wide open, and he was so thrilled that I let him choose out all the sweets he wanted, and he chose a variety.

I told Trey he could eat some of his candy as soon as we got back in the car, which he did. He was bouncing off the walls, jumping all over the couch, and sprinting around the house in circles by the time we came home. He was a whole different child.

Oh my God, what do I do? I stood in the middle of his zooming. What should I do? He's flying around the house like the Road Runner. I asked my mother, a nurse, for guidance. "Put him in the tub," she said right away.

So I put Trey in the bathtub, hoping that my mother's suggestion would work and that the warm water would relax him. Trey was still as crazed as before. In the bathtub.

Finally, Sheree called to check in, and I told her what was going on and that he had eaten a lot of sweets. "Oh no, you can't give him all that sugar," she said matter-of-factly. It makes him really agitated."

It was, without a doubt, a bonding event. Not just for me and Trey, but also for Will and myself. Apparently, there was still a lot for me to learn about child care.

"I'm expecting."

Will and I are sleeping in a rented Cabo San Lucas villa. It's the late summer of 1997. I'm twenty-five, about to turn twenty-six, and Will and I have flown down to Mexico for a break from work. We're both breathing heavily in post-passion, and I'm experiencing something I've never experienced before, and it's TERRIFYING.

Right there, freeze the frame. Let's go back in time a few months.

Will and I were approaching our two-year anniversary in February or March, and he was out of town working. We'd liked drinking together since I started dating Will, so I was back to drinking a lot. I dismissed it as part of our way of having fun. But one day I was confronted with the truth of how much was too much.

I had been staying at Will's house with my girlfriend Sidra while he was out doing film marketing. We drank white wine and split a bottle. I finished a second on my own when she took off. I was about to buy a third bottle when I came to a halt. I had this thought: I'm drinking by myself in the middle of the afternoon because I'm bored and lonely. You have a problem, Jada.

I went cold turkey at that point. There will be no more drinking. Sobriety felt nice for the most part—clearer, more robust, and more in sync with my body. I would have intense cravings for alcohol, but they would pass.

This coincided with my discovery that the birth control I'd been using—the depo shot—had a side effect of depression. When the extreme mood swings began, I realized it was time to try a different type of birth control. I wasn't worried because I thought I was safe after my last shot. I assumed I wasn't ovulating because I wasn't menstruation. That was accurate. The majority of the time.

My mother, an ob-gyn nurse and birth control expert, told me, "Don't fuck around, Jada."

How do you know you've just gotten pregnant in the split second it happens? If you've ever gone into a bank vault, you'll know there's a lock that looks like a giant round steering wheel, and as you turn it, it locks with a CLICK.

That's how it felt in my womb.

This is what I tell Will after he looks at me skeptically. And I say it again, "I'm pregnant."

He takes a seat. He has a look on his face that screams, "You must be crazy." He bursts out laughing. "Jump up and down," he recommends. "Stand on your head."

I'm too shaken to answer.

He phones Duane to keep making jokes about me thinking I'm pregnant before the kids had even stopped swimming. I'm crying while he and Duane are laughing. I can't stop crying all night. I'm certain I'm pregnant. I'm sure Will can hear my mental monologue: What the fuck have I just done?

Technically, we've just finished. However, becoming pregnant changes everything. It's not that I haven't fantasized about becoming a mother and tenderly bringing a child into the world. It's just that I wanted to plan ahead of time.

I went out and got ten pregnancy tests two weeks later. This was not to be overdone. It was methodical. Fawn arrived at Will's residence. I gave her five tests and gave myself five tests. Fawn failed every single test she tried. Every single test I took returned a good result.

Finally, I'm pregnant!

The beginning of morning sickness added to my bewilderment and worry. Or you could be ill all day. I was preparing for a role in Return to Paradise, a film starring Vince Vaughn and the late Anne Heche. I'm sure I came across as distant or cool since I couldn't stand straight for more than ten minutes without feeling sick. Following an incident, Vince made the remark, "Aren't you a peach?"

I couldn't fault him. I couldn't tell anyone except Anne, my homegirl at the time, that I was pregnant. I informed her in confidence, so she understood.

The level of dedication I witnessed with Marion and Gilbert, as well as Shirley and Grant, piqued my attention. Even with my wish to love and be loved in that way, I'd seen how husbands and wives take each other for granted—far more than loving and respecting each other. That was not something I desired. And I was certainly not prepared to make a lifelong commitment to God through a spiritual contract. This was a foregone conclusion.

But I had always imagined having a child. It wasn't unimaginable for me to be a single mom or have a close male buddy coparent with me. So why not? I had my own job and my own money. If I choose to be a single parent, I could do so. These ideals were as powerful to me as someone else's thoughts of walking down the aisle in a white gown. Of course, all of this was speculative. It was till it wasn't.

And I wasn't feeling prepared. But, now that I was pregnant, it was evident that, with or without a piece of paper declaring Will my husband, he was the father of my kid, and that was a type of "till death do us part" regardless.

I was able to listen to Will when he came to my side as I was resting on the chaise lounge I had installed in his bedroom—just like Marion's—once I realized that this tiny being inside me was having her or his way and had chosen us as parents. Will leaned in and proposed while I was lying there, attempting to relieve my all-day pregnancy sickness, stating there was no way I was going to have a baby until he married me.

I couldn't help but cry. His proposal was lovely and heartfelt, but I was terrified.

The mountaintop wedding was all I had at the time. Will, as usual, was preoccupied with work and didn't seem to notice the impending wedding. He normally preferred to make exceptional occasions into events, but he wasn't ready to express his thoughts just yet.

When I recounted everything to my mother, she was not impressed. "Jada, you are my only child," she sobbed. You must have a wedding."

This was a step too far. "I don't want to get married." I need to focus on what I'm about to embark on."

"You are my only daughter."

I attempted to see it from her point of view, but I didn't have the bandwidth. Putting on a wedding was extremely distracting at a time when I felt we should have been focusing on who we needed to be and what was required for a happy marriage. I was unwell, afraid, and lacked the energy or desire to make a wedding to-do list.

But it's up to Adrienne to make her case to Will. Will took her side as she sobbed on the phone, assuring her that there would be a wedding after all. Even though he didn't require a large wedding, he thought it was vital to have a ceremony with family and close friends.

Will and I decided on December 31st, New Year's Eve, and made plans for a small, intimate gathering in Baltimore, where Will was filming Enemy of the State. Details were kept under wraps to avoid an avalanche of reporters. The day before the wedding, we planned to notify the guests of the venue. Grandmother Shirley, my last remaining grandparent, was convinced we were doing this to confuse her so she wouldn't come.

I rejected in both cases because I wanted to honor my grandfather Grant Pinkett, the first man in my life who was completely devoted to me. I wanted the world to know that I had contributed to his legacy of love, which had helped me get to where I am now. It sounded like Jada Pinkett Smith. It was a good one.

As the date approached, my father expressed his desire to attend. I stated unequivocally that I did not want Robsol present. This may have appeared harsh, but it was all too much for him.

Will listened to what I had to say.

A strong commitment was made during that interaction, almost as if we were making an implicit promise to each other even before we went to the altar. In that moment, it was as if he was saying, "I trust you." And all I was saying was, "I love you enough that no matter what happens, we are going to work through it, whatever inevitable challenges come up, and for better or worse, we are in this for the long haul."

Our vow was holy, made without the intoxication of a fairy tale wedding ceremony. It was two people sitting down and being honest and clear-eyed with each other in front of God. Finally, I had my summit moment, while he and Adrienne got their wedding shebang. Everyone came out on top.

This talk would be significant for me in the years to come because, no matter what, I would find it impossible to go back on my word, given to him in that precious time.

Everything we'd have would be built collaboratively. That was a given from then until now. Divorce could have been inevitable without that pact, but it has saved us from irreversible conflict on numerous occasions.

The wedding took place at the Cloisters in Baltimore, which reminded me of a castle with its old-world grandeur. We had around eighty intimate friends and family members. My gown was cream velvet, precisely like Grandmother Marion's for her winter wedding. Will wore a cream-colored suit designed by Badgley Mischka, who also created my gown. Although I did not have bridesmaids, Fawn, my mother, and Aunt Karen all wore Badgley Mischka gowns.

Aside from the media attention and fuss, the wedding was pretty basic and down-home. Adrienne was overjoyed at her achievement of being Baltimore's top wedding planner. She was joined by the rest of my immediate family, my Baltimore homegirls, and Lyte and Jasmine Guy, who had flown in. Will's whole family and old Philadelphia friends, as well as his Fresh Prince castmates, were in attendance.

As far as shotgun weddings go, it was gorgeous, but we skipped all the niceties. Will and I chose to go down the aisle hand in hand toward Aunt Karen's pastor, Rev. Dr. Marvis May of Macedonia Baptist Church, whom we had met just a few days before.

Tra-Knox, a group Will was managing at the time, sang the Jodeci song "Forever My Lady" a cappella, and Will's friend Charlie Mack said he'd sing "She's Your Queen" from Coming to America when they were finished. That didn't happen, but our wedding was completely hood, which I loved.

I had mostly followed the flow of the day, but as soon as we were halfway down the aisle, I was overcome with emotion and couldn't stop crying. Straight up sobbing. I was both thrilled and sad, hopeful and terrified, triumphant and unsure. But I knew I was going to give this marriage my all, and I was going to offer my child the opportunity to have the father I'd never had.

We all partied together after our vows and brought in the New Year on a new beginning, and that's exactly what it felt like—a clean slate. Something changed the moment I said "I do" and we were officially husband and wife.

Will was suddenly my entire world. My heart had fully yielded. Hearing myself addressed as Mrs. Smith was strange, but it was a symbol I could finally accept as part of my new life.

I looked around at my family and friends and saw so much love. Trey's little darling self was seized so he could cut our wedding cake with us. I understood that my obligation to him had increased. He wasn't my boyfriend's son anymore; he was my bonus son, and that's exactly how I perceived him.

I felt a heaviness lift that I had been carrying for so long.

It was like something old had died within me, and something fresh had entered. I was at ease. It felt almost as if I had been standing on a precipice, anticipating what the fall would be like. I felt as if I'd landed unscathed now that I'd taken the leap. My worries were gone, and I had a bright future ahead of me, with the chance to start the family I'd never had.

Part III: Ride-Or-Die

Chapter 9: Little Gurus

My children have loved me as the best and worst of myself without hesitation at every level of their development. There was no flinching or blinking. They are my heart's most powerful instructors. I don't use the term "little gurus" lightly.

Trey felt deeply linked to me from our first meeting, and I rapidly became devoted to him. When Will and I married, I fulfilled my promise that if I was going to be the loving bonus mom to Trey that he deserved, I needed to put any resentments and misunderstandings between Sheree and myself behind me. I couldn't say I loved Trey without hugging his mother.

There was no manual for how the ex and the new partner should get along in the early days of my relationship with Will. It doesn't matter who wanted the divorce in the first place, because no one enjoys the prospect of being replaced. It might be especially difficult when the new spouse is acting as a guardian to your child at times. That can be disastrous. For my part, being the new partner didn't provide me with the sense of security that Sheree may have felt I possessed. Sheree would always be Will's first wife and the mother of his first son in my mind—experiences I would never share with him—and this made me feel like the alternate at times. The losing candidate.

After Will and I married, and as our baby's due date approached, I believed it was critical to move over any apparent rivalry between Sheree and myself. Will and I were committed to creating a blended family, and Sheree had to be a part of that equation for it to work. Trey was joint custody by Will and Sheree, and like many children of divorced parents, Trey split his time between the two residences. That is difficult enough, but the most difficult days are birthdays, holidays, and other special occasions. We wanted him to be able to celebrate with everyone he cared about, including his future siblings. I didn't want him to miss out on experiencing the fullness of family. I didn't want him to refer to his brothers as half or anything other than siblings. That's my younger brother or sister.

I was moved. The answer was always there. We both desired the same thing for Trey: a loving, harmonious household experience that neither of us had experienced as children. We both come from broken families and were reared by a single mother. We both had identical wounds. Our only challenge was putting aside our egos when we felt territorial, envious, or even nasty.

We gradually evolved from friends to allies and, much later, additional sisters. In the course of reconciling with Sheree, I was given the gift of meeting her mother, Pat, Trey's devoted grandmother. Pat and Trey were like two peas in a pod, and because she was with him so much, we got to spend a lot of time together. Pat welcomed Trey's brothers as bonus grandchildren as soon as they were born. Sugar Mama was so named because she gave the kids as much candy as they wanted, even when they weren't supposed to.

The more I thought about it, the obvious it became that I placed much too much reliance on material possessions to provide me with worth. This was due, in part, to the fact that they were a symbol of status for those of us who grew up in a world where having a significant quantity of the nicer things in life—whether shoes, bags, clothes, jewelry, or even food—seemed so out of reach. Trey's baggage was wanting to have every desirable cereal box in my cabinet at the same time and never feel deprived. My lesson was to let that go and assist Trey in developing his own sense of values in relation to his belongings.

To this day, whenever I walk inside Trey's closet, I see that he has only the bare necessities, which is consistent with his credo of acquiring only what I require. It's a lesson I'm still working on.

That was the last time I told him not to give his possessions away. Instead, we came to an agreement on specific goods that Trey would truly require, such as a good suit for important occasions. "Trey, I'm putting this suit and these dress shoes in your closet for you to use, but they are items that belong to me," I'd remark in those circumstances. Is that all right?"

This was a means of communication that Trey and I could both get behind. But, no matter what we gave him, I always made a point of emphasizing "This is yours," so he felt free to choose whether or not to keep it.

Trey reminded me that children are not carbon copies of their parents. They are distinct individuals with distinct values, strengths, and sensitivities. Trey had been the only kid for quite some time, so as my due date approached, Will and I made a concerted effort to find methods for Trey to feel included in the process of welcoming his new sibling into the world.

My pregnancy was far from uneventful. Those nine months were filled with both hardships and magic. In stark contrast to how difficult my first trimester had been, as soon as I hit month four, I became the happy I had ever been in my life. I felt calm, joyous, and tranquil in an unprecedented level, and I knew it was because of my child's energy. Before ever entering this world, my child possessed an openheartedness. My greatest concern was that I would squander that lovely energy through poor parenting.

This small being forbade me from eating meat when I was pregnant. The very concept of that made me sick. I used to follow a vegetarian diet but would occasionally eat meat. This baby demanded a vegetarian diet. Eating for two, I resorted to a high-carb diet, which gave me a little more than fifty pounds and turned me into a walking beach ball.

Dr. Gail Jackson, my ob-gyn, told me a few weeks before my due date that the baby wasn't dropping at all and that I would be two weeks overdue. There's still over a month to go! It was July, and I was so huge that walking was difficult and breathing was impossible. There were also bogus allegations in the newspapers that I was incapacitated due to a medical ailment. I couldn't blame the gossip. I would have felt the same way about myself.

I had no idea how to get my kid to drop and birth on time because the mysteries of parenting were already so enormous and intimidating.

A few days later, I got up from watching the US Open on TV and went for a walk outdoors to get some fresh air. I discovered some relief from the San Fernando Valley's July heat. The time had come for me to open my heart and gently implore my baby to come out: "Mommy loves you very much, but I really need you to come out." Mommy is having a difficult time. I cannot wait another two weeks. You're supposed to arrive on July 9th. Mommy is exhausted, and I desperately want to hold you. Can you help me with this? Please?"

There was no indication that the baby was ready to leave his or her happy place. My mother, fortunately, had decided to come stay with us before my delivery and then for as long as I needed her. I was happy to benefit from her years of experience as an RN in labor and delivery rooms. But she also kept reminding me that due dates were not to be trusted, and that if Dr. Jackson suggested the baby may arrive two weeks late, it was very possible.

The days passed at the slowest possible rate. I could hardly move by this point. On the evening of July 7, I had just gotten into bed, uneasily waiting for Will, when I heard a loud CHIME from the security sensor as he stepped through the door.

My entire body gripped with pain when I heard that sound. This had to be a contraction since I felt like I was splitting in two.

I summoned Will. He ran in as he yelled for my mother, who arrived in our bedroom not long after.

"I'm in a lot of pain, Ma." "I believe we should visit the hospital."

My mother quickly pointed out that if this was my first contraction, it was far too soon to go to the hospital. "The pain can't be that bad," she remarked, "you probably haven't even dilated yet."

"No, this is bad," I said emphatically.

I'd heard that if you weren't at least three centimeters tall, the hospital might send you home. We had a bit of a trip to Cedars-Sinai, and I didn't want to rush there only to be turned away.

Mom followed me into the bathroom, turned on the water, perched up on the counter to keep me company, and said that there was no rush and that I'd feel better once the hot water relieved the pressure.

There was no way out. The hot water only made me feel hotter, and the pain intensified. Mom suggested I do a deep squat as I got out of the tub, which is an excellent technique to relieve bladder strain. My water broke as I assumed a sumo wrestler pose, or so I thought as liquid flowed over the bathroom floor.

"Well, that's that," my mother exclaimed as she leapt off the bathroom counter. "It's time to go." She hurried out of my bathroom to get dressed while also summoning the rest of our army. "Will!" she exclaimed. "It's time!"

We ran into the garage a few moments later—me, Will, Adrienne, and our nephew Kyle, who happened to be staying with us at the time. With my pain levels at an all-time high, all I could think of was the cherry-red Bentley coupe with the tan suede seats.

I put my pregnant tail on the stack of towels and stuck my head out the window so it didn't strike the car's ceiling. Will drove so rapidly on the interstate that a trip that would normally take close to an hour took half that time.

I became really relaxed, even happy, once the epidural was delivered. After a few hours, Mom was by my side, watching the monitors, when she realized that the contractions were lasting too long and the baby's heart rate was falling, much to her chagrin. The worry was that the longer the contraction lasted, the more difficult it was for the infant to acquire oxygen, placing the newborn in danger.

Dr. Jackson proposed a C-section after further examination.

"No, no, no, I'll relax and ease these contractions." I do not want to have a C-section. I'll be just fine."

"Okay. Let me at least give you an episiotomy so you don't tear." She pointed out that the baby was large and I was petite. I, too, declined the episiotomy. MISTAKE!

The hours tick by. The night goes into the morning of July 8, and my child finally decides to make an appearance. My due date is still a day away.

My mother is holding one of my legs in the air as the nurse opposite from her holds the other. Will peers over her shoulder with a look I've never seen on his face—pure wonder. Dr. Jackson stands at the foot of the bed.

It's a first.

Will has never been in awe of anything. For a brief minute, I'm concerned that I'm misinterpreting his look and that something is amiss.

"We've got two more pushes, Jada." "Push hard," Dr. Jackson says quietly.

I'm relieved. Everything is going as planned. In her element, my mother joins in, pushing me, "Come on, Jada. "You've got this."

I spy Dr. Jay Gordon, the pediatrician I've picked for his natural approach to treatment, as I gather my strength for an extra-hard push. He confirmed my feelings: I didn't want my kid to leave my side after birth or to be given meds that weren't absolutely necessary.

So, Dr. Gordon has arrived to ensure that my newborn is healthy and that no one tries to argue with me about how I want my baby to be cared for.

"Jada, we're almost there. "Just one more push," Dr. Jackson exclaims.

This is the end. I take another deep inhale and exhale with a deep primal grunt as I push so hard that blood vessels pop in my skull. Then I hear...

"It's a boy!!!!"

My infant does not cry right away, which causes me some concern. Dr. Gordon carefully takes my son and examines him thoroughly. My baby's eyes slowly open, and he whines loudly.

Dr. Gordon hands our baby boy back to Will and declares, "He is perfectly healthy."

This makes us all feel better.

Will immediately brought our son to me, and I cradled him close. I couldn't believe how stunning he was. He was as peaceful in my arms as he was in my womb. I couldn't take my gaze away from his gorgeous face, and I felt so connected to him—more than any other connection I'd felt in my life. Will was beaming, and this bundle of love laying on my chest had me completely enthralled. Nothing compares to the miracle of bringing life into this world.

I still couldn't believe I was a mother.

We hadn't settled on a name yet. Will didn't like the name I chose for myself, Syre. "How can I be the Fresh Prince when my son's name is Sire?" Nope."

The next day, Will stepped into my hospital room after returning from the house. In his little incubator bed, our baby slept beside me. I was already half asleep, regretting my decision not to get an episiotomy. For the next three months, I'd be sitting on a doughnut.

Will had an announcement to make. "I know what I want to name him."

"What?"

"Jaden."

I took a breather. "Jaden?"

"Yes. He has to be named after his mother, based on what I saw yesterday. That's the first time I've seen anything like it. I'd like to name him after you."

I couldn't think of anything to say. I didn't know how to respond to this recognition, and I couldn't help but think, I'm not deserving of this. This youngster is just too unique to be named after me. This was my genuine belief. Even now, after giving birth to our kid, I couldn't accept Will's attempt to honor me.

"Sons want to be named after their fathers, not after their mothers," I finally said.

"His name is Jaden," Will stated emphatically. "Um, I hate to tell you this, but I don't think that thing is ever going to work again," he said, half-seriously, half-jokingly, as he pointed to my little cat, now a boxing glove with fourteen stitches on the inside and twelve on the outside.

It had already been decided. Jaden, my gorgeous kid, was to be named after me. I followed a Jamaican tradition by giving Jaden two middle names. Trey gave his younger brother Christopher as his first middle name, and I gave him Syre as his second.

Along with Jaden Will drove us all home slowly as I stared at this amazing being I already knew and thought, Welcome to the world, my little guru.

He had a gentle, accepting expression on his face. I guess that works, he appeared to say. He made no further protests and entered the room where his company was gathered. When I arrived about five minutes early to get him up at noon, I noticed him posted by the door, bag on, patiently ready to leave.

I dropped him off and waited in the car for half a day every day for two weeks, and at 11:55 a.m., he'd be ready to go, waiting by the door. The teacher came me on the last day and said, "Oh, Jaden is such a delight. He is really pleasant, although he does not socialize much. Everyone wants to get to know Jaden, but he doesn't interact much." I politely listened. "We'd love it if you guys came to the final picnic," she continued, and I agreed.

On the scheduled day, Jaden and I arrived at the picnic and found a bench to sit on. Jaden never left my side. Kids approached him and greeted him, and he was courteous in return but showed no interest in further interaction. When the teacher approached him and thanked him for being a part of the program, he nodded and smiled but remained seated.

That was such a telling moment, letting me know—this child has an unshakeable inner understanding. He retained his own inner protest, as if to say, "I'll be here, Mommy, and I'm not going to defy you." I'll be polite and considerate, but as I already stated... I have my circle of buddies. I don't want to be where I'm not supposed to be.

My son possessed a strong sense of self-determination. Even at that young age. This sweet, peaceful, self-assured child, standing firm on his feet and not bending.

Don't mess with Jaden's inner compass, and don't mistake his tenderness or generosity for a weakness. My job was to understand and strive for clear communication while never undermining his powerful quiet power. I'd only end up hurting myself trying.

Jaden's lessons that summer were eye-opening. He was never again left at an educational facility unless he chose to be there. From then on, he was homeschooled.

My faith in him and a lesson in patience were subsequently tested when Jaden asked to audition for the role of Will's son in The Pursuit of Happiness. I made a point of leaning in to the request because it was entirely Jaden's idea. Will and I were almost usually on the same page when it came to parenting decisions, and we were both leery about exposing Jaden to the risks of being a child actor.

My little Willow, oh my God, she was fearless and unafraid, even in the womb. She arrived in this world with a blaze of vitality, a mix of lightning and thunder, mega-sunshine, and the most compassionate heart. Her compassionate heart has been one of my biggest teachers since the beginning.

When we weren't sure whether we were having a girl or a boy during my pregnancy, Sheree told me she'd had a dream and wanted to share it with me. When we had a chance to converse, she vividly explained her dream, building up to the fact that she had seen my new baby and "in my dream, she was a girl." Not only that, but the tiny girl would have light hazel-greenish eyes like mine, "but lighter, and more cat-shaped."

I could stay strong in crisis most of the time, but I lost it one day when I was ready to drive Willow to karate class. She had entered the bedroom to say good-by to Will, but as she sprang for his arms, she slipped from his embrace and smacked her head on the corner of our bed, splitting her forehead open. Blood was gushing everywhere. Willow started screaming at the top of her lungs.

I felt the room spin and fainted, tumbling to the floor as my body essentially shut down. Will, thankfully, came into action and handled everything.

We were in the car in no time, Will was driving us to the hospital, and I had recovered enough to concentrate on Willow. I was broken when she looked at me and said, "Mommy, can you fix me and make it better?" It would take me years to properly accept whatever emotions arose from watching her in anguish. The lesson was that suppressing my own strong emotions meant denying hers or, worse, losing her entirely. That was incomprehensible. So I set out to learn as much as I could from her about how to mother both of us.

The Willow Wisdom approach is to feel through things and address the hurt rather than burying feelings under the rug. Willow goes through all of the heartbreak, all of the raw intensity, all of the outspoken expressing of her emotions, whereas I swallow everything and keep it moving. I get to observe her wonderful, dynamic paradox of vulnerability and bravery. Willow taught me that being vulnerable is a superpower.

Willow's first order of business as she learned to speak seemed to be to express the strength of "I love you." To this day, there remains a trail of "I love you" messages spread throughout our life, written on paper, folded up and put into notebooks, scratched on the wall (luckily in pencil), forever to be found as reminders. In her exquisite eight-year-old cursive hand, she would send me, her father, and other tribe members what I consider love letters—missives like this: Mom,

I love you! I consider myself extremely fortunate to have a mother that understands and does not judge me. Mommy, I adore you!

Willow, like her brother Jaden, has had a high level of independence since birth. Willow understood exactly what she wanted and went after it. During my pregnancy, I could sense her fierceness, as if she was getting ready to do her own thing, whatever it was. Interestingly, I didn't gain nearly as much weight as I did with Jaden, and within a month, I'd dropped it all and was back in shape in time to start shooting a movie.

Breastfeeding had a significant impact on how rapidly I lost weight. And I had planned to nurse Willow for as long as she desired. I didn't expect her demand for independence or her love of eating to appear so quickly and abruptly. Willow ate a plum when she was one year old. That was the end of it. She weaned herself in one day there and there. I'd never known a child to wean themselves all at once, in a single day. I didn't know what to think except, of course, my daughter would be starting her own flow at such a young age, just as I had done in my own manner.

Willow, like me, was born an animal lover. Every animal. When she was a toddler, her comfort with animals was on full display on a trip to an Australian child-friendly petting zoo where we were permitted to touch koalas and feed kangaroos. Jaden was about three years old at the time, and Willow was about a year and a half. Willow toddled right over to where the Cheerios were stored for animal snacking as I moved their two-seated stroller next to the kangaroos and helped herself to a small handful. She felt as safe and at ease among the kangas as if she belonged there. Jaden remained in his stroller.

"Do you want to get out, Jaden, and walk around and feed the kangaroos?" I inquired about him.

"Do you see his long nails, Mommy?" he asked, looking up at me and pointing to the kangaroo's feet. When I looked down, I noticed the kangaroo had razor-sharp toenails. I laughed at Jaden's gentle way of screaming "Hell no!" and "Why would you let Willow steal their Cheerios?" Keep an eye out, Jaden. I picked up Willow, slid her back into the stroller with Jaden, and we rolled out.

Willow desired more exotic pets by the time she was five years old. In the beginning, she caught garden snakes in our backyard. She desired to be linked to nature in a very different way than Jaden, who is perfectly content with simply walking barefoot in the grass. Willow was looking for a deeper primal connection.

At the age of six, she declared, "I want a pet tarantula, Mommy."

As a pet, a tarantula? Now, look, I believe in providing certain experiences for children in order for them to self-actualize. But a tarantula wasn't going to happen. "I'm not sure about a tarantula, sweetheart. Mommy and tarantulas don't usually go down."

Willow maintained her tarantula obsession until she visited a friend's pet store and was able to hold one of their new arrivals—a young red-tailed boa constrictor. She was overjoyed when she called me. "Mommy! I'd like to have a pet snake! I'm holding him now, and he's so adorable!"

I remained mute.

"Mommy, I want this snake so bad, pleeeeease?"

"Willow, those snakes eat live prey!" "Who's gonna feed it?"

"I am, Mommy," Willow insisted.

As I sat on the phone, I had to ask myself, "Am I going to let Willow miss out on this experience because of my own fears?" She is not afraid of snakes. She's holding one right now. This was her link to her basic self and nature. I was captivated by her courage, and as a mother, I wanted to instill it in my children. My convictions reminded me that being a woman in this world necessitates bravery and fearlessness. Why should I refuse her lessons from this snake because the streets taught me?

That's when I caved. Willow delighted in bringing home a lovely baby red-tailed boa. We gave him the name Beauty. The first feeding was unforgettable. I'll never forget how terrified I was that we had to put live mice into the boa's cage, and how Willow turned to me with her hand on my arm and explained everything. "Mommy," she started, "this is how life works." It's part of the natural cycle."

I fell in love with the snake while seeing Willow. Beauty was purportedly her pet snake, but I grew close to her, and as Willow developed other interests—like the two turtles she brought home that we discovered were tortoises and may survive us all—I adopted Beauty as my own. I soon acquired more snakes since I was fascinated by them. True. Snakes respond to subtle and dramatic vibes and energy, and your relationship with a snake is all about tuned in. They showed me how to do just that. However, without Willow, I would not have gotten that appreciation or skill.

Will is a wuss. He never grumbled. I believe he found it amusing as the animal world swiftly expanded from felines and dogs to reptiles and more, even saying, "It's Noah's Ark over here."

Being able to observe Will and Willow's bond has allowed me to witness something I would never have in this lifetime, something money cannot buy—the love of a father full of paternal sweetness. I will never have a father I can call Daddy, and I will never know the kind of love that only a father can give to his daughter. For me, it's a delicious heartbreak. Every time Willow calls her father Daddy, it melts my heart and makes me grateful for the blessing of having a loving father on whom she can rely. Will's affection for his sons remains the same.

The fact that I gave my children the father I would never have given them has allowed me to find peace with my own daddy issues as an adult. It is a part of adulthood to be able to rejoice when your children receive a gift that was not intended for you. That is parenthood's selflessness.

I've had to remind myself at every stage of their life that my little gurus are having a completely different experience than their parents. We wanted to shield them from suffering and hardship, but we also wanted them to be free to follow their ambitions on their own terms.

At the same time, I was always clear that any success any of us achieved belonged to all of us. I drilled that from the beginning. "Everyone benefits from your success." Nobody in this family achieves anything by themselves." I preached it in a variety of ways. I didn't want any sibling rivalry and wanted each child to understand how important it was for them all to go through this thing called life. And if blood can find a way to respect, consider, and love one other, there is no stronger link. According to my findings, based on my own experiences and observations of other families, getting along with siblings is not always a given. As Willow, Jaden, and Trey's siblings, I wanted something unique.

Nothing I discovered as a mother compared to the power of unconditional love. My earliest views of it came before the kids could even speak, when we had a physical connection while sleeping side by side every night. Call me superstitious, but having them by my side as newborns and toddlers was crucial to me as their defender, given the many mysteries that swirl in the night. Later, I learned that familial sleeping is common and promoted in Africa.

Jaden and Willow slept with me as infants and continued to do so for many years. Will needed a vacation from this sleeping arrangement when Jaden was about six and Willow was four, which was understandable. I had even made a separate, gorgeous love nest for us two grown-ups in our bedroom, replete with a domed ceiling full of twinkling stars, to give us our own space. However, the kids eventually took over that room as well.

Will finally said his bit one night. I'd just gotten into bed when the two youngsters climbed in next me. "Tonight, why don't you two try sleeping in your own rooms?" Will remarked as he entered the room. They objected, but Will stood fast. "Come on, come on. Just give it a shot tonight. You're becoming older."

Will brought Jaden and Willow to their rooms, and they were both quite sad. My heart broke, but I thought Will was correct. They were growing elderly.

When I awoke early the next morning and opened my bedroom door, I saw both of them huddled up and sleeping in the hallway. This was their polite protest to express they would NOT accept not being by my side at night. And I wasn't about to take anything for granted. I'd never felt so loved. Will, of course, gave up on that.

Soon after, they both made the decision to sleep in their own beds.

I've done my fair share of blunders as a mother, to be sure, but one thing I do know, warts and all, is that I love my children fiercely—deeply and unreservedly. And I have a feeling they have always known how much I adore them, even if I can't put it into words. Above all, LOVE is the most stable foundation we can provide for our children.

Even when they were small, I was taken aback by Jaden and Willow's need to be with me all the time. Perhaps because my young mother was more like a big sister, I didn't feel the same desire to be with her all the time, and I was surprised when my children objected to being with other people. My mother, called Gammy, who gave herself that moniker as soon as she became a grandmother, and Mirna, who I referred to as my "parenting assistant" and who became like a second mother to the kids and a member of our family, were the only exceptions.

To this day, all three Smith children enjoy spending time with their parents, and we do as well. There aren't enough words to convey how much Trey, Jaden, and Willow's love has meant to me. They assisted me in seeing the possibilities of my worthiness as a result of parenting. Eventually, they broke down my walls enough that I had to consider—There must be something really amazing about you, Jada, if your kids adore you this much.

Chapter 10: Swallowing the Key

The importance of perspective cannot be overstated.

Will had made that remark on one of our first dates, when he pointed to the glass on his left that was also on my right, and it remained with me. At the time, I felt he was showing me how he navigated the world. I soon realized that the principle could be applied to our relationship.

It is not our fault that we have unrealistic expectations. The fairy tale of idealized love is responsible for the numerous false notions that exist today. We must think alike if we love each other. Right? If you truly love me, you must be aware of all my needs at all times, without my having to inform you. Right? And if you fail to meet these expectations, I have the right to disdain you, treat you as an enemy, and search elsewhere for what I require because you have chosen not to provide it to me. Right?

No way, no how.

We rarely pause to assess or even recognize the harm done to us by romanticized ideals—whether in movies, songs, TV shows, books, advertisements, or other people's glossy descriptions of their wonderful lives. We enter committed relationships as if we knew how to build healthy, truly loving partnerships, with those happily-ever-after fairy stories in our heads.

I'm sure that as a new wife and mother, I would have given more room to my own history if I hadn't been caught up in the dream of how my Prince Charming would make all my suffering disappear as he rode me off into the sunset. I would have admitted that I had only recently attempted to distance myself from the Hollywood lifestyle in order to create a smaller, more private one in Baltimore. Or perhaps I would have been more deliberate in my decision to discontinue treatment once I was off Prozac—not long after a succession of tragic losses that I hadn't processed.

As a graduate of the University of the B-more Streets, I was ready to distance myself from Will when we disagreed in the beginning. Will could talk circles around me at the time, so it irritated me when I felt he wasn't listening and was being disrespectful. Once, during a heated disagreement, I let off an F-you, battling in the style I was most comfortable with.

Will was having none of it. He basically said, "I can't be in a relationship with you." "This will not work."

He ended our relationship right away. His argument was that, given the abuse he had witnessed between his parents as a child, and how things had quickly escalated from verbal to physical, he was unwilling to engage in this type of heated engagement with me.

"So you're going to break up with me over some words?" I inquired.

Will replied, "Yes."

I attempted to think about his point of view over the next week. My experience was different from his, but flinging words was one way I protected myself in certain circumstances where I felt endangered.

Nonetheless, I could imagine a more courteous approach to communicating.

We were just separated for a week. Will, on the other hand, had established an important border. And he did it in such a way that I couldn't help but notice. It was one thing to use profanity to communicate ideas or perspectives, but quite another to use it in a personal attack. My eyes were opened to the fact that words can be weaponized and as brutal as blows. Similarly, disrespect can lead to emotional violence, which is another reason to be careful with your remarks.

Will stated clearly what he was willing to put up with. "If we are going to be together, we can't do that to each other."

I concurred. I never cursed at him again after that episode. Not for decades, at the very least.

Our decision to refrain from using profanity or rude words or tones resulted in better communication. However, the unintended result of our more "respectful" discussions was that they were frequently lacking of genuine emotional expression and were sometimes unduly academic or analytical. Imagine having to sit down and talk about the times when some women flirted with him in front of me while remaining calm, even-toned, analytical, and detached. This habit protected us not only from discussing but also from experiencing genuine emotions.

Will and I had quite different ideas on the trappings of celebrity by the time we were married and had children. Early in our relationship, ripples of our differences appeared, but I ignored them because the ride was all-consuming.

Will was on his way to becoming the unquestioned box office champion, having already spent more than six years on TV screens in millions of people's homes across the world. Being kind to fans was part of his work ethic, but it became increasingly difficult to go places just with our team to have a good time. As a result, we attempted to go out when things were less crowded so we could move around freely and have fun.

Everything was going well until a group of admirers spotted Will and started sprinting toward us, virtually in hysterics as they sought to get close to him. It sounded like a raucous, eager stampede.

When I looked up at him, he seemed perplexed by my outburst and could only ask me to calm down. Because of our varied vantage points, we experienced two distinct physical perspectives. Will, at six-two, could see enough of the crowd to know there was no actual threat. I'm five feet tall on a good day, tiny in comparison to everyone running at me, and all I could see in my rush of adrenaline was the incoming rush of bodies. Screams were all I could hear as hands reached across my face. Will managed to calm the horde, and we all got on with our lives. But I was frightened.

To him, I had overreacted, despite the fact that I had been in a full-court-press trauma response. To me, he was underreacting and refusing to comprehend how being mobbed would make me feel like we were all under attack.

Early in my career, I learned to build my own comfort zone by addressing the photographers and stating, "I'll give you the pictures you want, but you have to back up." Give me 20 feet." I was fine as long as they didn't come right up in my face. "No problem, Jada," was the customary response. As a result, the paps and I had mutual respect.

But crowds, fans, and paparazzi were all part of the package. And I'd have to learn to deal with it. I also realized that just because we were in Hollywood didn't mean we'd forgotten where we came from. I mean, I was living the ostensible dream, and one of my best friends was murdered, despite being music royalty. And it was here, in adapting, that Will and I agreed that our role was to provide for and bring as many people as we could along for the voyage. This is what some people call survivor's guilt.

This meant that whenever someone in our network needed help, he and I were frequently the first people called. Those unexpected calls would come in during the hours when you knew it wasn't good news. People in need of bail money, assistance following an accident, or finances to pay for a funeral after their kid was slain. Or perhaps someone was ill and need the services of a specialist. Someone was in trouble and needed to get a lawyer. We had the means to assist and felt bound to do so if we could.

We were like so many individuals in all walks of life who, despite their best intentions, find their worth in overextending themselves on behalf of others to the point of becoming incapable of self-care. Will and I were both naïve in this regard.

With both of us juggling careers and families, there was even less time for us to check in with each other and address our differences in depth. Every attempt to reconcile our opposing viewpoints resulted in our pushing the can down the road and Will's declaration, "We'll get to that later." That became our relationship's theme tune.

Everything went downhill quickly. We lacked the commodity of time.

Will was on his way to stardom, and I was putting in my own gas, trying my hardest to live up to the impossible standards of being a great wife and mother. I had no one to blame except myself. I had not only joined up for this voyage, but I had also taken my seat within my own gilded cage. The terrible key was then swallowed.

Our family had outgrown our Westlake home by the time Jaden was a toddler. The guest rooms were always full of Will's relatives and friends who had been by his side for years. Charlie Mack, for example, lived with us before Jaden was born and used to blast Chico DeBarge at five a.m. almost every morning... until we had a talk about it. The best part is that Charlie is like my older brother, and we could always chat about anything. He smiled and even looked startled that he had been so clueless after only a few words. I never heard Chico as the sun rose again after that.

Will deferred to me on the majority of decisions concerning our frantic household. We were most likely the only Black couple in our neighborhood at the time, which made for some unusual interactions with the primarily white service providers, who, although kind, seemed unaccustomed to being hired by young Black homeowners, renowned or not. Most of the time, I handled whatever situations arose, but if there was something I truly needed Will's opinion on, I'd ask. That's what I did when I contacted him at work after an exterminator incident.

A switch inside me switched to preserve mine at all costs. I took a glass blender jar off my kitchen counter and lifted it, warning him, "You better get the fuck out of my house!"

The man quickly backed out of my kitchen door and left. What shocked me the most wasn't him, but where I was willing to go. That area within me hadn't been activated in a minute, but it was still ready to blow. The other side was that I was hurt that someone I had been okay with could be so disrespectful and breach my own safety in my own home.

His quick remark indicated that he was in the midst of something. He basically stated that I had handled it and that we will discuss it when he got home.

Then I did what I always do. I took command, became tough, and concealed my desire for reassurance. I said goodbye with a short "Cool," and we hung up.

We didn't discuss it later. We really should have. It should never have been acceptable for me to ignore someone who was making me feel violated in my own house, so much so that I felt compelled to back down. It should never have been acceptable for me to let Will brush over it, either.

Had I explained myself clearly? In retrospect, I'm almost certain I didn't. That is an admission. Even now, it's tough for me to convey how I truly feel at any given time. Any sign of weakness makes me feel uncomfortably exposed.

So many talks and facets of our existence slipped our minds. We had to learn on the fly how to deal with the challenges of raising a family, operating a household, and coordinating the intricacies of continuously being on the go. As more and more passengers sought to board, ours was a classic case of learning to fly an airplane while still developing it.

Oh my goodness. I enjoy throwing parties, but this quickly became an annual event that I had to plan, as the guest list grew to include every celebrity in Aspen at the time.

Everyone else simply saw the glitz and glam of our existence. People were rarely aware of what was going on when forty-plus family and friends went on a Christmas holiday. Or how difficult it was to get up everyone on New Year's Eve 1999, my second wedding anniversary, when the world was going to end and all I really wanted to do was be quiet with my husband and family, and fly off to D.C. to spend the night at the Clinton White House.

It is unavoidable for everyone willing to ride on someone else's bullet train to become disoriented while traveling to that person's destinations. It happens to a lot of people, not just in the entertainment industry, but in all walks of life.

I was quiet and had to think hard when Harvey stated this. It was impossible for me. I recognized that Will Smith was the huge brand name in Hollywood. But so was Denzel Washington, who was eager to be a part of the project. Although Will and I worked on projects together back then, they came up spontaneously. We never worked together as a group to get things done. The trap seemed obvious to me. If I granted that request on this project, I knew it would be expected the following time, and the next time after that, by everyone else. I withdrew the film with remorse. I refused to gamble with Will's success.

Our most significant point of disagreement was our perceptions of what happiness included. Will was living his dream, which meant I was living mine through him. He couldn't figure out why I was always upset. Why would you desire anything, he reasoned? Consider the life and opportunities I give for you, all the things we get to have, do, and be.

Chapter 11: Wild Banshee

The narrative I'm going to tell you has many entrance points, but I wouldn't be able to honor my grandmother if I didn't trace the primary thread back to my time in Baltimore. Marion wanted me to be able to explore worlds other than my own so that, no matter who I met later on, we could find some common ground. From the classical composers I heard in her house to the R&B, disco, classic rock, and even country my mother loved, from the reggae and Caribbean rhythms played at my aunt Sondra's to the club music and old-school hip-hop I heard on the dance floor and at the skating rink, from the 1980s alternative bands Pac, John, and I obsessed over all the way to my exposure to hard rock and heavy metal in the home of Unc, my openness and love for all kinds of

R&B may have had a stronger hold on my soul than other musical genres, but metal/hard rock held a distinct type of strength and control over me. It called to something basic within me. So much so that I'd always wanted to do it myself, to unleash that energy within me and truly rock out. Tichina Arnold, an actress and singer, stated in my birthday video that she believed there was a white man trapped inside me someplace. Metal pulls out the fierceness in me, and that genre of music provided a safe haven for its expression. When Guns N' Roses came on the scene when I was fifteen, I was captivated. My childhood ambition was to be the first female Axl Rose. Suzi Quatro, Doro Pesch, Joan Jett, Heart, and Stevie Nicks were among great female rockers I adored, but there weren't many Black women on the rock scene at the time, to the best of my knowledge. I didn't find a Black woman who could rock like that until I was introduced to the London-based band Skunk Anansie, led by Skin, a fantastic bad-as-hell lead singer. Of course, Big Mama Thornton, Memphis Minnie, and Sister Rosetta Tharpe were rock pioneers, but their contributions as Black women are frequently overlooked.

Hollywood never seemed to be able to tame me, and I refused to be tamed. Part of that entailed being myself, regardless of who I was sitting in front of. That might be a double-edged sword. Warren Beatty later offered me a kinder perspective when I provided suggestions on his Bulworth script.

This was one of those screenplays that Warren wanted to keep private, so I had to go to his office to read it since he was considering casting me. After that, I told him the truth: "This is not realistic." It struck me as culturally inauthentic. "I can't do this."

Warren was impressed, however my tone and approach as I continued to analyze his writing may have been off-putting. Warren patiently listened, his gorgeous smile on his face. He could tell that my abrasive tone, combined by naked honesty, wouldn't necessarily go down well in a town full of egos.

Warren invited me to lunch after I realized the movie wasn't for me. In other words, he suggested that it could be in my best interests to soften my stance a little. He said I was talented, amusing, and engaging, but that I could be aggressive at times. He was asking me to let more of the delight hidden beneath my hard façade shine through.

This was the first time anyone had explained it to me in such a nonjudgmental manner, and I liked it. He didn't condemn me for being who I am; he was simply asking me to be open to showing additional sides of myself. He made it apparent that I didn't have to compromise myself by softening my edges. That was reasonable. Taking his advice into consideration, I knew I needed to find a place outside of Hollywood for the wild banshee within, the one who didn't care if she was soft or delicious.

It was time to move on, to explore a new world. The world I needed appeared out of nowhere.

When I fall in love with a passion, I fall hard. And then I go all in.

That's how I felt when Will brought home the Matrix deck. He was the filmmakers' initial option to play Neo at the time. Though it initially appeared to be a comic book, the graphics immediately captivated my imagination and had me salivating mentally. I was a die-hard anime fan, and I believed that if they could carry off what was imagined on paper, this film would be one of the best of all time.

The Wachowskis cast the largest and most diversified casting net possible, which was one of the most hopeful and amazing aspects of the movie for me. Before Hollywood jumped on the diversity bandwagon, the Wachowskis recognized the value of diversified representation that went beyond ethnicity. They were expressing their worldview as directors, which went beyond heterosexual white folk living in an apocalyptic future.

After Laurence Fishburne was cast as Morpheus, the cast became even more diverse, which made me want to be a part of the production even more.

I felt like the role of Trinity was written for me, and I was overjoyed when the filmmakers liked my audition and invited me in for a chemistry read with Keanu. This was going to be a piece of cake. I mean, I was a major Keanu fan. What do you think? We had no chemistry during the reading. There are none. Zero.

I was completely taken aback.

When I don't get a position I truly want, I usually think that I would have been a better choice. I can't think of anyone who would have made a greater Trinity than Carrie-Anne Moss. She was the most awesome. I'm here to tell you that this is one of the few roles I lost to another actress, and I couldn't have played it as well as Carrie-Anne did.

So it appeared that being a part of the Matrix phenomenon was out of the question. That is, until the Wachowskis decided to start a Matrix franchise and create two sequels to it.

I was not going to pass up this opportunity and would later admit that my remark was a bit of a stretch. This meant that once Willow was born, I'd have to drop the baby weight and get back into shape quickly. It was going to be difficult, but I told them that I would be prepared. Willow, on the other hand, kept me honest by arriving two weeks early on Halloween.

I increased my typical gym workout while pregnant. I was scheduled to begin shooting for three months at the end of November. I needed to be prepared, and I only had a month.

I doubled down in the gym when Willow came, engaging on one of the most difficult training regimes of my life with the one and only Darrell Foster—the same superstar fitness and combat trainer who helped Will prepare for his role as Muhammad Ali. I started my motion capture employment in very good shape, with baby Willow and toddler Jaden, my homegirl Fawn, and Gammy, who would be on set with me all day. Every hour on the hour, my mother would bring Willow from my trailer to the set so I could breastfeed. Whatever baby weight I'd gained vanished quickly, thanks to Willow's nursing.

But after working up to pressing 10 plates on each side of the leg machine and bench-pressing 175 pounds as one exercise, I acquired fifteen pounds of muscle in no time. I'd never been so ripped in my entire life. Darrell got me so conditioned over my two-year journey with The Matrix that we considered me competing as a bikini bodybuilder. I was taking gymnastics class, fighting with the cast, and lifting weights with Darrell. Working out became my way of life.

"Next week, at the Viper Room, Sharon Osbourne is coming through to hear you play," I never anticipated to hear a couple years into my metal music adventure.

What's going on?" "Yeah, Sharon wants to check you out for a possible place on the Ozzfest tour."

My bandmates and I were all clear that Sharon—Ozzy Osbourne's wife and the powerhouse behind Ozzfest, the world's largest rock and metal summer festival—would make the decision based on the performance she was there to see that evening.

Of all, we'd only been around three years, and I didn't want to get my expectations up that we'd be able to participate in the event. We'd have to go out there, give it our all, and hope that our varied metal sound made the cut.

This was an incredible opportunity for which we had worked very hard.

When we first started, it didn't take long for me to come up with the name Wicked Wisdom. "Wicked" was a nod to my West Indian ancestry, meaning "dope, excellent, or even unusual," and "Wisdom" was the state obtained after absorbing and practicing the deepest truths. Songs spilled from the depths of my heart and bowels, like if they'd been waiting for years to be heard. Titles, lyrics, and melodies came easily to me and filled notebooks, pieces of paper, and even napkins.

Miguel Melendez, my boss, seemed perplexed during one of our initial meetings about my new venture. Miguel, a big bro, collaborator, and valued adviser on many aspects of my acting/producing jobs, said respectfully but skeptically, "Metal?"

He had to declare right away that he was unfamiliar with how to maneuver in the metal music industry. Rather than discouraging me, Miguel hired Dennis Sanders, a promoter and manager who had previously worked with Papa Roach, knew the terrain, understood my concept, and began booking us in every venue he could.

Dennis would schedule us here, there, and everywhere, intending for us to gain experience. Wicked Wisdom traveled wherever there was an address, or a location on a map claiming to be an arena/club/bar, or a cornfield with a falling-down cabin in the center of it.

There was a logic to the madness—you can't really tell what works or doesn't work until you get out there and play. This resulted in a lot of trial and error and raised eyebrows. Still, it was that spirit that helped Dennis book us a two-month stint as the opening act for Britney Spears' Onyx Hotel Tour in early 2004.

The music critics were perplexed. The old-school rock-and-soul segment was well received, but reviewers couldn't figure out why we were opening for the reigning Princess of Pop. They weren't altogether incorrect. Again, we soon learned how to put on a show and develop enthusiasm in front of large people. We learned considerably more because we were on a large tour with so many moving parts.

One of my favorite parts about traveling on a tour bus overseas was getting to share the experience with Jaden and Willow, who were six and four at the time. Will would join us at various points, depending on his schedule, but most of the time it was just me and the kids. After our rehearsals, I'd have a lot of downtime between gigs in different cities. That meant the kids and I could hang out, they could take music lessons from various band members, or we could go sightseeing.

When we initially saw this place as we drove up, I thought there had been a mistake. It was practically smack dab in the middle of a cornfield. It appeared to be a large shack. That is, a makeshift shack. I'm in the middle of nowhere.

When we stepped in, the place was packed to the gills with white youngsters who had no idea what to make of us. We could also see by their numbers that they were ready to rock out and throw down, despite their reservations. That was nothing new to us.

The lighting also appeared to be rigged incorrectly. Someone had sprinkled several giant work lights around, the kind you see at night for road maintenance, but they didn't do much to illuminate the vast space.

A gate divided the stage from the audience below in some indoor settings. These gates were supposed to be effective as a barrier between performers and rowdy members of the audience, so no one thought to climb up onto the stage. The youngsters were already pressed up against the gates in front of the stage at this shack/club, anxious to see what we could accomplish.

Once the play began, I became increasingly enthralled, as did the audience, and I lost track of myself. The audience responded to what they were hearing by forming full-fledged mosh pits and slamming into one another with abandon. I jumped up on the gate to get closer to the crowd, like I was accustomed to doing. I completely forgot about the open wires in the ceiling, went up to grab a bar for stability, and nearly electrocuted myself.

Throughout my metal journey, I learnt about the myriad white Americans from lower to middle-class neighborhoods that feel unheard and abandoned by a country they believe has abandoned them. Some blame those who resemble me, while others blame the government for being corrupt.

By living in the belly of the beast for five years, I also grew to comprehend prejudice on a deeper level. We are afraid of what and who we do not know. When we get past the anxiety, we have to let go of some of our prejudices, which I did after witnessing the deprivation of the white hood and white poverty firsthand. In this country, I observed parallels between impoverished Black people and poor white people, because poverty deprives all people, regardless of color, of their dignity and self-worth.

Seeing the shared struggle of the poor, working, and middle classes helped wash away some of my preconceptions and misunderstandings. This unexpected cultural immersion taught me a new lesson about how art may cross the gaps that divide us.

The Viper Room—leather booths, jewel-tone lighting, somber and sexy—was very luxurious in comparison to most of the dumps where we'd been playing. But that wasn't what made this night unique and interesting. Sharon Osbourne, as promised, arrived to hear us play on this night.

Before we approached the stage, we took a moment backstage to connect as a group, say a prayer, and express our thanks. Then I said, "Let's go fuck shit up."

Passion spreads like wildfire. There was never any doubt about that with us. I'd improved a lot as a vocalist, knowing how to sing and growl at loud volumes without losing my voice. Our nu-metal music worked well with my voice and expressiveness, but where I felt most at ease was in my showwomanship. I enjoyed absorbing the audience's excitement and producing a spectacular performance. In addition, my band was BADASS.

That night, I had a terrific time, which I thought meant we had a great concert. Dennis grabbed me from backstage and led me to Sharon's booth once I was offstage.

It was no coincidence that both Jaden and Willow would feel at home in the universe we explored and pursue their own musical paths as a result of this encounter. Jaden discovered his own passion for rock 'n' roll and tour busses, and Willow took it a step further by learning to play the guitar, rock stages, and unleash her own wild banshee.

Ironically, the first official announcement that Wicked Wisdom would be performing at Ozzfest came just as I was leaving for a live interview with BET. I couldn't help but tell the audience about the wonderful news.

The word immediately traveled throughout the metal scene, and the retaliation was swift and intense. I would eventually master the art of letting the most ludicrous and nasty rumors roll off my back. Listen, gossip magazines and websites may be filthy and discouraging. But nothing beats true threats like "We're going to stomp her, rape her, cut off her head, and dump her naked body in a ditch," especially if you're a live performance.

I tried to take the venom in stride, but I didn't always succeed. Thousands of comments on Ozzfest Web forums ranged from predicting I wouldn't make it through the entire tour to declaring Wicked Wisdom would ruin Ozzfest forever. According to a single post, "Wicked Wisdom will be pelted by every loose object on the Ozzfest grounds." Someone said, "This is going to cause an f-ing riot … bring your steel-toed boots."

The death threats were so detailed, and so many, that the head of my security detail was firm: "We are suggesting you don't go." It's far too risky."

I'm not going to lie—I was shaken. But, when it was suggested that I turn down this chance due to people's ignorance, I refused. "I'm going," I said simply.

Will understood how significant this was to me. Although he was anxious about what I would face, he recognized it had to be my decision and supported it. I would have reconsidered if this were now, in an era of severe racial violence. And I certainly would not have driven with my children.

Recognizing everything that my predecessors had endured in far more traumatic circumstances than being a Black metal band on Ozzfest was the determining factor. This was not the Middle Passage, or escaping on the Underground Railroad, or walking through the doors of a white school flanked by federal marshals, as six-year-old Ruby Bridges did in 1960, or even facing the hate hurled at Black entertainers and musicians who traveled across a segregated America at the risk of their lives, merely trying to earn a living and share their gifts. No, attending this summer festival was not one of them.

We knew there was an audience out there for us because of our forefathers' efforts. So I increased my alertness and hit the road.

We first encountered the actuality of the dangers in Camden, New Jersey. Before our performance, I was informed that there was a large number of neo-Nazis in the audience. The boys and I conferred, put on our gear, and said, effectively, "Let's do what we do."

JC and an army of his homeboys were working the festival to confront the neo-Nazis. JC, a six-three, 225-pound, baldheaded, tatted, Viking-looking white male, knew we'd have some difficulties on tour. If you were to judge a book by its cover, he appeared to be more hardline than any of those neo-Nazis. When we were told what was going on in the audience, JC assured me, "That shit ain't going to fly like that." I had no cause to be skeptical of him.

"BOOOOO!!!" Before we even hit a note, the air was filled with the roar of outraged naysayers. We began to play, and the "Heil Hitler" salutes began to come. Before we finished the first song, I noticed JC dash from behind me and perform a Herculean stage dive into the Nazi mob, openly bashing his body into them.

His vibe was quite strong. What's going on? If you want to mess with someone, fuck with me.

And guess what they did? They were terrified. Those men had a lot of heat to hurl at me, but they didn't want any smoke from JC. That day, I discovered that the majority of those males who were acting so hard and full of hatred were actually cowards. JC was always telling me, "Any man who treats a woman that way is a sorry-ass motherfucker."

No matter how chilly or nasty the vibe was in Camden, I made it my business to stroll through the throng before and after the event, to remind myself that there was nothing to be scared of, and if someone in the crowd wanted to hurt me, well, here I was. The majority of people didn't even notice. People paid their money to have a nice time, at the end of the day. We'd done well if we could deliver it and possibly alter some hearts and minds.

One of the most refreshing elements about being engaged in the world of metal and stepping outside the velvet rope was that no one gave a damn about the machine known as Hollywood. They had real life to consider, which helped me stay focused on the same.

I tell you what, having the opportunity to see masterful bands like Black Sabbath and Mastodon perform live every day gave me some of the best times of my life, as did sharing the stage with Arch Enemy's dope female lead performer at the time, Angela Gossow, who killed it at every performance. I learnt a lot and made a lot of friends, including the crew from Bury Your Dead, Brent Hinds from Mastodon, and many others.

I discovered a lot in common with folks from many backgrounds who I met at the time. Not every performance hit the high notes, but there was nearly always a connection that we could acknowledge— Man, we have shared this moment, this slice of life, and it was fun. Even though I used to refer to myself onstage as a wild banshee, it wasn't for the sake of being wild and out of control. No, I got to shake off the domestication that had encircled me for years.

I craved the wild banshee that used to haunt the Baltimore streets at midnight. The one who enjoyed strolling on the precipice of danger. So many of us abandon our primordial callings in order to make a living, be the responsible daughter or son or PTA member, and follow rules that make us worthy in the eyes of others. There are many outlets other than metal music that we may all pursue in order to escape the boxes we've placed ourselves in.

Our inner banshee wants us to allow her some breathing room—to rattle her cage, to get dirty, and to get away from all the societal pressures to be acceptable, proper, and, frankly, flawless. If left unchecked, perfectionism and its more hazardous relative, romanticism, might cut off your oxygen supply.

I am grateful for everything. The success was that, whether you loved our music or not, you couldn't question Wicked Wisdom's heart.

Just as Ozzfest was wrapping up, we received an incredible opportunity to be one of Guns N' Roses' opening acts for their 2005 European tour. It was beyond comprehension.

We barely had time to catch our breath before we had to hit the road again. During my little respite, I flew to San Francisco, where Will and Jaden were about to begin principal photography on The Pursuit of Happiness.

As soon as I arrived, I found myself at a fork in the road. Although I urgently wanted to go out with Guns N' Roses, there was no way I could leave Jaden's side while he worked on this tough film. Will would not have the bandwidth to be his father on-screen while also being Daddy off-screen in his first significant job. Not for a film that told such a compelling story. Will required my presence to ensure that Jaden received the emotional support he required for this event.

I walked out into the San Francisco night air, seeking my own counsel, and thought of Jaden and all the time he'd sacrificed, traveling all over the world with me so that I could live my dreams, whether it was going to Australia for The Matrix for a year and a half or being away from all his friends to travel on a tour bus with me so I could perform with my band. It was now my turn to make a sacrifice for him. I opted to decline the chance to open for Guns N' Roses.

We nevertheless released our second album and performed at some wonderful places, including a tour with one of my favorite bands, Sevendust, and a performance at the Download Festival in the UK the following summer. The band was then placed on hold. I never looked back and regretted any of those choices.

For over five years, I had been pursuing a dream of becoming a rock hard in a way that nothing else could. I had gone as far as I needed to go when I stopped, even though I could have gone further. My children were maturing and beginning to develop their own lives and pursue their own interests. I didn't want to miss seeing them soar. They'd accompanied me on my flight, and I wanted to accompany them on theirs.

Part IV: To the Exiled Lands

Chapter 12: Surrender

What is the significance of the index finger?

The more I reflected on my bizarre dream, the more I was reminded of spiritual principles I had learnt. I had forgotten that the index finger signifies the ego in many spiritual practices. The most difficult impediment in my quest for complete surrender in peace was my raging ego, not anybody else's.

Sure, I had left aside the pseudo-guru's know-it-all attitude, but now I was convinced I was on my path to sainthood. At this point in my life, I'd rid myself of every habit in my arsenal; I had no relationship to retreat to; and I was practicing abstinence from alcohol and sex in a rigorous manner like I'd never done before. This left me staring at my ego's werewolf in all its machinations, appetites, and deception. Despite this, I'd barely scratched the surface of who I needed to be.

Clearly, I was unqualified to ride this alone. When the pupil is ready, the instructor appears, according to the Buddha. And I looked for teachers everywhere.

We met in person or through their pages, and I sat at their feet, heart wide open. Many religious writings I'd previously studied were revisited, as were the worn pages of my spiritual guide Clarissa Pinkola Estés, everything by Pema Chödrön, and a new find, Reclaim Your Heart by Yasmin Mogahed. I searched into illuminating passages on what it meant to live with Jesus, to be devout as portrayed in the Quran, stories from the Torah about the many aspects of God, and Sufi mystics' knowledge. Marion had laid the groundwork for me, and I was putting it into action.

My attention then shifted to studying more about holy women from many religions, such as Fatima, the daughter of the prophet

Muhammad (may Allah's blessings and peace be upon him), and her devotion to her family and God even in the face of persecution. I heard about the majestic Indian saint Anandamayi Ma, who was born with the purest heart and spirit, so much so that sitting at her feet allowed people to experience the Divine. Then I learnt about Tahirih, the first female Bahá' martyr, and the Sisters of the Beguine Order and the Sisters of the Holy Family, Black Catholic nuns in New Orleans. Rabi'a, a female Sufi saint,'s devotion to Allah helped me grasp the necessity to build a bridge between God's love and my heart. Discovering the soul food offered by amazing and unheralded women provided me with the spiritual nourishment I'd been seeking.

Ram Dass, American-born yogi and author of Be Here Now, exposed me to a difficult concept that became one of the most useful spiritual axioms I learnt early in my studies.

That kind of love is impossible to achieve when the ego raises its index finger. But what if you happen to meet someone who has attained that state?

I had the fortunate opportunity to find out just before the pandemic.

On one of my last days in Singapore, where I'd been shooting a project with Gammy and Willow, my brother-in-law Harry Smith, Will's younger brother, inquired. The two of them were leaving for the United States, but I was considering staying longer and even going on my own.

Harry and I were particularly close during this period since we were both transitioning to new lifestyles. It was a difficult stretch for us. We kept in touch on a regular basis.

"Singapore, we're almost done. But I'm thinking about going to Vietnam before returning to Los Angeles."

"Really? You already know Thich Nhat is there."

I'd never expected to meet Thich Nhat Hanh, a respected Buddhist monk whose YouTube videos had proven therapeutic for both Harry and me. I became a student of his after reading his book Living Buddha, Living Christ in the late 1990s.

"I think he is still in Europe."

"No … Jada, he's there. You should track him down and pay him a visit."

"Harry, are you positive that he's in Vietnam?"

"I'm positive."

That, however, changed everything. Where can I find Thich Nhat Hanh in Vietnam? There was no doubt. I had to make an attempt to see him. I answered the phone and went for it.

Taking a vacation like this alone myself was something I hadn't done in a long time. Being alone in an unfamiliar place—detaching from previous life ideas—can be a harrowing experience, given that it would be just me and my ego. Nonetheless, I was ecstatic.

Because it was rainy season in the north, my intention was to visit two cities in central Vietnam before heading south. I'd travel to Hue to visit Thich Nhat Hanh's monastery. I didn't have confirmation, but even walking around the grounds of where he formerly lived would be meaningful.

Ben, my security guard, was the ideal guy to accompany me on this trip. He is a former Navy SEAL of Samoan heritage who is laid-back and without bluster yet is exactly who you want by your side when things go wrong. Ben and I arrived in Hi An, a seaside town with numerous five-star resorts. The air was hot and humid, but it wasn't oppressive. Even in the midst of the chaos of getting off the plane and being greeted by customs, there was a calm that put me at peace. In that tropical temperature and peace, my body relaxed and I began to unwind.

On our way to the hotel, I noticed a massive Quan Yin statue and made a mental note to go see it. Quan Yin was a well-known person to me because she is highly adored in Vietnam. As is Buddha, who establishes a lovely balance of the Divine's male and female energies. Another site I was able to visit in this area was a Buddhist temple located in a deep mountain cave where wounded troops were sent to recover during the Vietnam War. Hiking is always enjoyable for me, but after the long trek up the mountain, entering that temple within the cave and experiencing the power of worship there was transformative. I increased my embracing of this season of rebirth that I was in inside the cave—often a symbol of the heart, the womb, or a cocoon, as in a place of rebirth. Being alone was not a punishment, but rather a necessity.

Vietnam itself has the feel of a temple island. The mood is pleasant and inviting, with an unmistakable swirl of devotion in the air. The gravity I'd been carrying for so long seemed to vanish after a few days. I'd never been in an atmosphere that so opened my heart and lowered my barriers, making it all the more impossible to conceive such a brutal, horrific conflict taking place among all this beauty and tranquility.

When we got in Hue, where we were staying at the aptly called Pilgrimage Village Hotel, I discovered that we were only five minutes away from Thich Nhat Hanh's monastery. Even though I wasn't sure if he was there, my excitement was evident.

Ben later knocked on my door on the evening of our arrival. "You won't believe this," he began, in his usual dry monotone, but with something enticing beneath his words.

"What?" Like a kid on Christmas, I said.

"We got into a conversation when I asked the woman at the desk about getting a tour of the grounds, and I told her that you admired Thich Nhat and had been following his teachings for a while." She then informed me that he was in the monastery grounds."

My heart pounded faster. "I gotta see him, Ben."

He smiled, amusedly patient. "I'm looking into it." Every night, she visits the convent. She's going to see what she can come up with."

I had to commend Ben. He was just as determined as I was to see this through.

I shut the door and knelt in my chamber, praying for the opportunity to be in Thich Nhat Hanh's presence.

The wheels of potential began to turn the next day. Ben and the hotel lady took me to the tearoom, where I met Nina, a lovely bald woman who was starting her journey to become a Buddhist nun and would meet that evening with a nun from the monastery who was assisting her. Nina (and the group she was with) urged me to remain and see the nun in the hopes that it would pave the way for me to meet Thich Nhat Hanh.

To do so, I had to go through a number of gates. Unlike in other situations when doors would open quickly for a celebrity or a spotlighted person, I knew I would be scrutinized more than others as to whether I was honest in my desire to meet with such a holy man. His health was also taken into account.

The nun from the monastery arrived that evening in her brown gown and began speaking with Nina and her party. I was introduced shortly after. Keeping in mind that no one knew English, the young girl from the hotel did her best to translate as I conveyed my fondness for Thich Nhat Hanh's teachings. Following the encounter, the young girl from the hotel smiled and told me that the nun wanted me to come to the convent. "Tomorrow."

Take a deep breath. "Tomorrow?"

"Yes, it is arranged." Nina, her friends, and I would roll together, she added.

When the allotted time arrived, I was brought to a portion of the monastery where I was greeted by a young nun who informed me that I would be meeting Thich Nhat's right hand, Sister Chan Khong. Sister Chan entered the room, also gorgeous, bald, and dressed in brown clothing, and I knew her from Thich Nhat's films and talks. She radiated warmth and strength. We discussed why I was there, and she explained how a desire to grasp the essence of love had influenced her trip. She seemed to be reading my inner biography.

Sister Chan then handed me an autographed copy of her book Learning True Love, which I kept as a lovely keepsake. I felt as if I had passed through the final gate after we vibed for a while more. She rose up and said she'd take me to meet Thich Nhat Hanh.

I was to learn that women were not typically permitted to access the monastery's men's side, where Thich Nhat was, but that an exception would be made for me because I would be entering with Sister Chan, Nina, and a small group of other dedicated sisters.

My pulse was racing as Sister Chan motioned for me to walk by her side. We followed the paved walkway through a grove of mature trees that added to the tranquility of this 1800s monastery. We soon arrived at his location, which was just outside the courtyard. When I first saw Thich Nhat Hanh, he was seated comfortably, his eyes closed, similar to many Buddha sculptures I had seen.

He was sat in a wheelchair, indicating that his health was deteriorating, and I could tell he wasn't saying much. But, thanks to the sister's gesture, I was able to approach him and bow at his feet, expressing my thankfulness and feeling his Divine energy. Nothing compares to the presence of a spiritual teacher. I experienced an automatic cleaning, a spiritual cleansing. It was stunning.

I remembered Thich Nhat Hanh's words, "There is no greater communication than silence," as I surrendered to this moment. That stillness is the language of the heart, where the tranquility and purity of love that transcends all rational and sensory comprehension can be found. And I was fortunate to witness this personally from the holy master himself.

That was the lesson that filled my heart and will endure a lifetime when it was time to raise my head and lift myself to my feet.

Soon after, I began studying the Gita (the Bhagavad Gita, one of the most revered Hindu writings that I had never studied) with Jay and Radhi on a regular basis. Jay introduced me to Bhakti Tirtha Swami's teachings, a Black swami from Cleveland's hood. How could I have gone this long without hearing of him? When Jay gave me Bhakti Tirtha Swami's book Spiritual Warrior: Transforming Lust into Love as a present, it literally changed my life! I became hooked with Bhakti Tirtha's teachings, watching everything he had on YouTube and reading everything he had written. Here was a Black man from Cleveland explaining his spiritual transformation journey, complete with numerous problems that I could connect to.

I increased my abstention after reading Bhakti Tirtha Swami's book Surrender. Beyond abstaining from sex and drink, I went deeper, letting up of material excesses (buying only for basics), including frequent fasting into my practice, and avoiding violent TV and music. Clarity and emotional sobriety were the objectives. Aside from the occasional use of colorful language, I became a sort of urban nun.

And then Jay asked me the pivotal question: "Would you like to meet my teacher, Radhanath Swami?"

I needed to take some deep breaths. I couldn't believe Jay was giving me this chance. Radhanath Swami, whose lectures I had previously attended, is one of the world's most revered Bhakti swamis.

My first thought was, "I am not worthy!" But that was old thinking that I was attempting to dispel.

My lessons with Radhanath Swami started right away via Zoom. This occurred during the global shutdown, and while he lives largely in India, he was temporarily in his birthplace of Chicago. My fears dissipated in the brightness of his wonderful grin the moment he came on the screen in his beautiful saffron robe. Even through technology, his energy had an instantaneous warming effect. Swami, an American-born son of Jewish and Eastern European immigrants, began his spiritual path as a child and decided to devote his life to Krishna in his quest for enlightenment. A scholar who having immersed himself in the study of several religions, he could impart knowledge from any of them in a single session. A Quranic quotation, an Old Testament or New Testament passage, the biography of a Hindu saint or a Sufi teacher might float from the top of his dome. I was astounded. Swami was in his early seventies and had such a sharp mind and an elastic heart that I learned simply by being in his holy presence and as a witness to his mastery of Divine truth from all these various faiths.

Swami was the perfect teacher for me. He taught me that the path to deepening one's surrender intersects with the path to comprehending what it means to forgive. After several Zooms, I finally admitted, "Swami, I'm having such a difficult time with forgiveness."

"You know, Jada," he said with all his might, "forgiveness is humbling ourselves before God in the face of all that we have done, and being willing to change and let go."

Hmmmm. A part of me wanted to deny or limit this reality by claiming, "I'm not talking about forgiving myself, I'm talking about forgiving others." But I sat silently because I felt Swami had something else in store for me.

"God's love is infinitely forgiving." Let go of the past's limitations. In our humility, we recognize that we can only seek refuge in God's pardon." He went on to gently point out that once you undertake the effort of forgiving yourself, it will reveal to you that you have little to forgive in others.

It was evident from this presentation that our human condition—in our sins and struggles—evens the playing field.

My heart rate increased. In that moment, I realized I was no different from everyone else who needed to be forgiven. We're all just trying to do our best. He made it apparent that rather than focusing on someone's misdeeds, we should focus on their ability to change, while also creating loving boundaries for ourselves and becoming a well-wisher. That is all we have been asked to do.

When I explained to Swami that spiritual recovery wasn't easy in Hollywood, he said the "Holy Woods" may be as effective a teacher as a cave in Tibet. Sacred wisdom emerges from everyday life, such as while doing the dishes, filling up a résumé, or coping with media overload, and it can even appear when you're having fun. To my amazement, golf was that enjoyable outlet for me, through which so many sacred lessons could flow—many of which were amplified when I got the opportunity to be given a golf lesson by the one and only Tiger Woods for his TV show.

Standing next to Tiger's ease, kindness, and degree of mastery instantaneously shattered my ego and allowed me to surrender to the game itself—which, to me, is analogous to the game of life. Who knew golf could teach you to let go of all thoughts of winning and losing in favor of simply being present and playing one shot at a time?

During the spring of 2021, I resurrected the spirit of the little girl I used to be, standing on the high-diving platform, terrified of jumping into the frigid water of the rock quarry below but unwilling to give up. That was the metaphor for recognizing it was time for me to leave Gammy's guest room, where I'd been living for nearly a year, and move into my own house.

It was time to plant my life as a garden of my own possibilities. That meant allowing my mother to have her own garden and having the bravery to create my own home.

Bandit, a pocket Frenchie gifted to me by Cesar Millan for my 49th birthday, would accompany me. I adore this dog, just as Cesar predicted. Bandit has no concept how small he is. He has a lion's heart, and you must earn his trust. He can chill hard and play hard, and he wants to be at my side at all times.

My key requirement choosing a house was its location, so that I could live close to my children and my mother, which narrowed the search. After nearly a year, I received a phone call from Miguel, whose wife, Lauren, had found a house they thought I should see.

I refrained from disregarding his suggestion. Miguel and Lauren were attempting to assist me at a moment when I was actively working on being willing to receive assistance. Besides, it was in the same neighborhood where I'd been living, near my people, and had everything I wanted on paper.

I made the appointment and went to visit the house despite my reservations. I was used to seeing a nicely photographed web presentation of a house that was far less attractive in person. So I braced myself for another letdown. What I discovered when I arrived surprised me. The house was quite open, situated in nature, with lots of wide windows and a view of the hills in the distance, and it was even lovely in person. It was beautiful yet simple—an aesthetic that allowed me to concentrate on what was important. It was a place where I might find love, connection, patience, and rest. It also included quarters for Trey, Jaden, and Willow in case they ever needed to do what I had—return to a maternal haven for some respite. The kids came to visit the house and enjoyed it as well. They were actually more excited than I was.

Before making the purchase, I sat down with myself for a serious powwow. No one welcomed my anxiety, anguish, sorrow, or doubt to join the conversation, which went something like this: Jada, you're about to buy a house. You will be formally leaving your previous life behind. Are you prepared to face this?

I took a big breath and responded, "I'm prepared."

I acquired my own apartment as a fiftieth-birthday present to myself, and set about furnishing it in a way that felt tranquil, like a warm hug.

I was in the Bahamas with my entire family and many friends to celebrate Jaden's birthday in July 2021, two months before my fiftieth birthday. I awoke one morning, alone in my bed, with hair all over my pillow for the last time. That was the day I raised the white flag and gave in to a decision I had been putting off for a long time.

Willow had shaved her head for the second time in her life not long before. She was onstage when she chopped it off, and it was a protest as much as a gesture of self-love. At nearly twenty-one, she was coming into her own as a creative force and serious rock musician. My darling. She looked stunning with or without her hair.

Willow had never pushed me to shave my head, but after witnessing all of my ups and downs, she decided it was time.

I decided to accept my hair loss as part of my spiritual journey. God would be the last arbiter. In a state of deep thankfulness, I addressed the Great Supreme, saying, "Great Mother/Father, if you want my hair, you can have it." In appreciation, I give you my hair. I'll offer it to you with a smile. You've given me so much, and if my hair is what you want in return, have it.

The more I considered my blessings, the more grateful I became for my challenges. They had given me the opportunity to grow closer to the Divine and learn how to submit. So I shaved my head and, strangely, felt even more lovable and worthy.

My baldness had become a sign of a covenant between God and myself.

Millions of people around the world, both men and women, were suffering, being bullied, and even contemplating suicide as a result of far worse cases of alopecia than mine. In comparison, my alopecia was minor. I wanted to share my story if it could encourage them and bring their challenges to light. Indeed, I was welcomed into a new group with love and acceptance, which I could reciprocate.

In honor of my new life and a significant birthday, I decided to throw my own party. I hadn't organized a milestone birthday party in all the years I'd been married to Will, so this was new terrain for me. And this year, for the first time in nearly three decades, it was very probable that Will would not be there to celebrate.

The prospect of approaching fifty had seemed so foreboding in my earlier years, but I'll never forget waking up on the morning of my actual fiftieth birthday, in my own bed, alone, in my own house—with Bandit on the floor next me—and feeling so full of wonderful joy just because I was myself. I could enjoy all the warm honey inside of me on my fiftieth birthday. I didn't require a new car or a costly piece of jewelry.

I was the gem. This journey, with all of its difficulties, had been worthwhile.

I took a deep breath, opened my heart to myself, and let my most thankful tears fall. I begged for wisdom in carrying this feeling with me through each new season, in the darkness and in the sunshine. I went into the bathroom, looked in the mirror, pointed at myself, and exclaimed, "Damn! "You fifty, bitch!" she exclaimed, laughing.

My party was held at my parents' house. And everyone in the family was present, even Will. He and I exchanged a fist-bump, and it was as if he was saying to me, Wow, look at you, congratulations. He had always supported my independence and was pleased to see where I was in life. I'd been able to construct an old-school skating rink for the festivities, a remembrance of a time in my life that had provided me so much joy. The celebration was tiny and held outside because it was still COVID-19, but the music was flowing and the laughter was loud.

Ellen and my RTT team planned a spectacular 50th birthday celebration for me, complete with shout-outs from friends and recognizable personalities from my time in Hollywood. They even got Toni Braxton to come out and sing "Happy Birthday" to me. Willow then outdid herself and surprised me by organizing a Wicked Wisdom reunion and playing one of my favorite Wicked Wisdom songs, "Bleed All Over Me."

My life was going full circle in front of my eyes in real time—so precisely that it was almost strange. Trey and Jaden capped out the event with the most heartfelt birthday greeting ever, leaving no stone untouched in terms of affection.

I was fifty years old and had finally found my way home.

Chapter 13: The Holy Joke, the Holy Slap, and Holy Lessons

Will and I had collaborated on philanthropy, business, and a variety of artistic endeavors throughout the course of our many years together. Will and I saw no need to part ways in our artistic and commercial collaborations when we decided that our marriage would become more of a life partnership, with family and holidays always being a constant. When we came together in that fashion, we were fervent admirers and believers in each other's abilities, extremely yin and yang, and it worked. The same differences that brought us together also resulted in remarkable magic.

It was in this context, not long after Sundance in early 2018, when I was a member of the festival's U.S. Dramatic Competition jury, that I made a strong recommendation to Will, who was due to play Richard Williams, father of Venus and Serena, in King Richard. There was no director to be located. I had a strong feeling about Reinaldo Marcus Green's film Monsters and Men, which I had seen at Sundance.

"You should meet Rei," I urged Will during a chat about the ongoing search for a director for King Richard. He is a very talented director, and I believe he has a talent for this."

Will followed my advise and watched Rei's film. Will, to my delight, agreed with me that Rei would be ideal for King Richard. Will then asked whether I would join him as an executive producer. He also requested my assistance in ensuring that the voices of the great Black females in the ensemble were properly conveyed, particularly the mother of Venus and Serena, Oracene Price, whom I admired and whose exquisite strength I believed needed to be a key part of the story.

Will's offer to bring me on board was polite, and I accepted.

I knew this character was in the greatest possible hands the day I saw Aunjanue Ellis read the part of Oracene in our living room. She portrayed the role so naturally, so strongly. Aunjanue, who had an impressive body of work, was awful to the bone in every subtlety. I was almost envious of her innate charisma and the outstanding caliber of her talent.

Will and I had a falling out before production started, which was a result of us attempting to navigate our separate lives and distinct requirements. I decided it would be best if I were removed from the film.

Will resisted, stating he wanted me to be a part of a film about topics we both cared about: black/female representation in a sport that rejected so many women of color; the value of family; the trials of parenting; and the universal force of endurance.

"But I don't want my name on something that I didn't participate in fully."

"You found Rei, you assisted me with the script, and I know this film will be special." I want you to be a part of the history that this film will produce."

I ignored it, and life carried on.

As awards season neared, I was pleased to see the film's numerous nominations and, of course, I was delighted and excited for Will when it became evident that he would be the frontrunner in the Best Actor category at the Oscars. The primary prize was getting the film nominated, but winning after two previous nominations (Ali in '02 and Pursuit of Happiness in '07) would be icing on the cake.

This coincided with a change I noticed in Will. He had just finished filming Emancipation, which had been a psychological challenge for him. Playing that character scared him to the point where he sought treatment, allowing him to begin to unravel everything that playing Whipped Peter had brought up for him. During the process, Will suggested that we take measures to return to treatment with new counselors. At first, I refused, but things changed when I met Don Rosenthal and Ishmiel Lounsbury. These two individuals and their approach would change my life.

I was pleasantly delighted when Will asked me to accompany him to the numerous award presentations in early 2022, culminating with the Oscars in March.

We have been there for each other at every memorable time in our life together. I was grateful for the gift of this opportunity and the continuation of our relationship in this form. After all, we had been legally married for six years despite not living together as a married couple. However, our return to treatment and his offer to stay by his side throughout awards season indicated that we weren't ready to give up everything just yet. We still had an unexplainable bond, an attachment that wouldn't let go. That couldn't be let go of.

My response was, "Of course."

So there we were, at the Oscars, living out Will's prediction that King Richard, with six nominations, including Best Picture and Best Actor for Will, would make history. And, as the rest of the world can attest, we did make history—just not in the way we expected.

This is simply a small portion of the backstory. There's more to it. There's a lot more.

My eyes rolled back. May I explain?

When Chris came out to present an award, made some jokes, got a lot of laughs, and decided to milk his time onstage like a comic, he saw my bald head and ad-libbed: "Jada, I love ya, G.I. Jane Two, can't wait to see it."

He couldn't help himself, just as I had predicted, and I rolled my eyes.

It wasn't because of the poke at my alopecia, but rather because of the others I'd met whose conditions were far worse than mine. That was, indeed, a pretty light joke, as many have noted, but it had nothing to do with me. I was irritated that most people don't understand how devastating alopecia can be. My heart shattered for the countless people who live in humiliation, for the children who committed suicide as a result of being tormented and taunted by their classmates. And now, in all its political correctness, the Oscars were telling the world that it was okay to make jokes about a woman with alopecia?

It was depressing. And I didn't take it personally. I was offended because the condition of alopecia was being made fun of. I knew I'd be alright. This was simply another day in the salt mines of our world.

My eye roll was merely me reacting truthfully and being... human. I didn't want to pretend anymore. After all—really, Chris? Do we have to go through this again?

Did it surprise me afterward that a slew of pundits would point to my eye-rolling as proof that it was my fault—you know, she gave Will the side eye and forced him to go up on the stage to smack Chris? No, I was not taken aback. Some of it surprised me, such as the suggestion that I could have stopped Will as soon as he got up from his seat, or instructed him to sit down and relax and leave Chris alone.

The vitriol came faster and furiously than I had imagined in the following days.

It's nothing new to blame the lady. And I was clear on it. It was simple to tell how the flawless Hollywood megastar had met his doom due to his defective wife. The patriarchy relies on blaming Eve for humanity's demise. The Adam/Eve dynamic was not necessarily on exhibit during the Academy Awards, but consider the context: women are progressively being excluded in some form. What's tragic is that many women have become the gatekeepers of this marginalization inside the patriarchal system, and are active players in humiliating and criticizing women.

I have to point out how strange it is that a woman can be entirely to blame when a male, any guy, does a heinous deed. How can a woman be both unimportant and guilty at the same time? It's an intriguing puzzle that will blow your head.

When it came to the Oscars in 2022, I had to consider the popular narrative of me as the adulteress wife who had now driven her husband insane with the command of one look. I have to accept responsibility for my role in perpetuating that false narrative. I also had to laugh at the thought that the rest of the world would think I had that much power over Will Smith. If I had that much power over Will, Chile, my life would have been very different during the last three decades. The truth!

When Will returned to his seat and Chris stayed onstage while snippets from the shortlisted documentaries were shown on the screen, the night's uncertainty increased. Everyone in the room appeared stunned. As the video played, Chris, who had moved to the stage's edge, noticed me in the front row next to Will and remarked, "Jada, I honestly meant no harm."

Will growled back at Chris, expressing his displeasure with Chris's conversation with me.

I couldn't take Chris's apologies and tossed my palm in the air, saying, "I can't right now, Chris, this is all about some old shit."

The action then returned to the stage, as Chris returned to reveal the winner, Questlove for Summer of Soul. A commercial break was taken following his acceptance. Denzel Washington and Bradley Cooper approached Will and crowded together, attempting to ground him.

For the next several minutes, I sat alone, attempting to find my own stable foundation, and was grateful for the men gathered around Will, because I was at a loss. Allow the men to handle this. I remained motionless and present, waiting to be called upon.

During the following commercial break, Will's publicist Meredith and my publicist Karynne came to our seats to discuss the next steps. Meredith had just returned from backstage and informed us that Chris had left the building and would not be pressing charges.

"Press charges—for what?" I inquired.

Meredith corroborated what I had missed: Will had made contact with Chris, who had not ducked, as I had assumed.

In disbelief, I stared at Will. "You actually hit Chris?"

Will nodded and murmured, "Yes," shocked that I hadn't seen the instant of contact.

I paused for a moment to regain my bearings.

We didn't know whether we were coming or departing in the fog of it all, even though we could have fled. Given our history of dealing with disruptions of this nature, we did what we knew to do: we moved through and attempted to return to normalcy as soon as feasible.

That, in my opinion, was how we all reacted to the events of that night in that room. It was a unanimous response: "Let's get back to normal." Nobody said, "Leave," or, "Omigod, what have you done?" Everyone became disoriented as a result of The Slap's fog.

Various groups of folks came over to check in throughout each ad break. Lupita Nyong'o, who was sitting just behind me, was one of the first to speak to me. "Are you all right, Jada?" she inquired. I'm very sorry."

I attempted to reassure her that I was fine, despite the fact that I was reeling and numb at the same time. Then came Nicole Kidman and her husband, Keith Urban, who are always so nice and generous in these situations. I comforted them and thanked them for their thoughtful care.

During another break, I was sitting alone when I looked up to see the one and only Ramsey Naito rush to my side. "Jada, I'm here, are you okay?" she knelt alongside me. When I saw Ramsey, my veneer crumbled sufficiently for me to admit that I had no idea if I was or wasn't. Tiffany Haddish then joined us, and Queen Latifah followed suit. This made me feel... chained. At least enough to dispel some of my skepticism.

Ramsey subsequently informed me that she had never seen me so alone and alienated, except on my fortieth birthday ten years before. The difference this time was that I was able to stabilize myself in the storm and find the inner strength to keep my head up. Will was my main concern.

I can't tell you why he did what he did, but it had everything to do with Will's own personal battles, which played out on a global scale.

And for the first time in six years since our divorce, I knew I would be there for him in this storm as his wife, no matter what. I hadn't felt this good in a long time. I would not desert him, nor would I fight his struggle for him as I had done so many times before. This was his fight.

Other emotional subplots converged for me during the 94th Academy Awards, which I couldn't untangle in the moment. What happened on that stage was a tremendously difficult, challenging, and painful event for everyone involved, including the audience. Without a doubt. It was agonizing and frightening to see a hero have a human moment as his trauma was splattered all over the room for all to see. It shattered the romantic notion that if we achieve enough, we will be free of our shadow. Seeing that kind of dispute between two Black males on a "white" stage was upsetting, as was seeing a Black guy insult a Black woman on a "white" stage. Once again.

Furthermore, women of color are almost never defended. As a result, even amid the clamor of people ready to blame Jada for The Slap, I recognized women from all walks of life privately yelling, "Fucking right! 'Bout time!"

A little echo of that sentiment reached out to me as well, making me feel—Thank you, Will, for defending me. But I was also aware that he was defending more than just me, and most of it had nothing to do with me.

Will was blamed for stealing the magic of a night that should have been remembered for fantastic wins for filmmakers, actresses, and other legitimately gifted artists being given their due. I took solace in the knowledge that there was no blood on the stage, no firearms drawn, and these two affluent guys would walk away unscathed, with no police intervention. This is not to lessen the humiliation of the confrontation that evening, but knowing that fame and stages don't keep you safe, it made me feel better that these two were able to walk away, injured but safe and alive.

Will, it appears, was caught in the snare of his own handcrafted gilded cage. He turns out to be human. As are all of us, including Chris.

And here's what ten years in the shadow valley had taught me: Everyone is in pain. harm people, as the phrase goes, harm people.

We frequently end up knocking against each other's hurts on the route as we seek our way. Welcome to the human condition. I was learning not to take anything personally.

I realized at the end of the Oscars live broadcast that it wasn't my position to try to steer any ship. My responsibility was to be a loving presence for myself and Will. There was no way to fix or avert the impending storm. The way out was the way through, and this night marked the opening of yet another undiscovered door.

One of this night's Holy Lessons was how to exercise unconditional love. All of the painful past of our complicated life together faded away. Will was going to require my assistance. I knew that those who had declared their affection for Will would abandon him. I understood exactly how he felt, and I knew he didn't. My heart ached for him, but I couldn't prepare him for what was to come. The only thing I could guarantee was that I would not abandon him. We arrived together and were going together. We were all in it together. Period.

Ride-or-die, Bonnie and Clyde, summon all the idealized versions of every outlaw nonsense you can think of. This was where my thoughts were. When all the nonsense between Will and me is said and done, this is what I do! I'm a ride-or-die kind of guy.

This night demonstrated to me that conflict can intensify love and compassion. It is simple to love someone in ideal conditions. But what if someone decides to develop a comedy program full of lies and unjustified insults? You love them as God loves them, and you tell yourself that when people are hurt, it could be because they believe lashing out will make them feel better. Is it true that I've never been there? No, it does not. This is when compassion and well-wishes come in.

As tough and challenging as the Oscars 2022 events were for

EVERYONE involved, I refer to them as the "Holy Slap" and the "Holy Joke" because of all the Holy Lessons to be learned for all of us.

In the ensuing media frenzy, I realized I was no different from any other Will Smith hater or critic. Will's charming behavior was the only thing I was willing to accept and appreciate. In his shadow states, I didn't know how to love him. The Holy Slap taught me how to walk hand in hand with Will, with all the bats and gremlins who had been banished deep into his darkest exiled realms, and to be a torch of love for him until he could find his own.

It takes a lot of practice to walk in the shadows with a loved one, but it is the cradle of unconditional love.

My personal shadow walk was the Holy Joke. Chris had already injured my feelings, and it was like rubbing an old wound when it reappeared. And, as much as I wanted to hang onto my grudges, I'd realized that doing so would harm me more than him. I'd seen a different side to Chris than his harsh jokes, and I couldn't turn back the clock. He deserves my attention and consideration, regardless of how he choose to drag me through the stages. That is his problem, not mine. From spirit to spirit, he is my brother, and I would not have been able to accept this message so fully if it hadn't been for his Holy Joke.

The Holy Slap taught me the significance of learning to love Will in his shadow, how to love myself despite so much misunderstanding and hostility, and how to love you, dearest reader, regardless of your thoughts on me, Will, our family, our marriage, or the Holy Slap. You have the right to think whatever you choose, and I will still love you because you are lovable and deserving by Divine order.

Be blessed. That is correct. Your will be done.

Chapter 14: Putting the Crown on My Heart's Queen

I've been fascinated by the mystery of magic since I was a child. From the earth magic in my grandmother's garden to the love magic that has carried me through my life and that I have been able to give with my loved ones.

This is most likely one of the reasons I am drawn to ayahuasca and its mystical, magical, healing powers. It leads you to self-love and the beauty of Divine love. Ayahuasca creates doorways to hidden planets inhabited by the language of love and magic. There's an explanation for this, since when indigenous South Americans met as tribes to drink the aya brew, their tribal ceremonies for healing included a wish to access the power of the unseen world where their ancestors roamed.

It bears reiterating that ayahuasca is not the sole path to magic, however it is a medicine that can assist you in discovering your inner transformational magic. It is a medicine that has worked for me, but it is not a medicine for everyone. Do you know what the most potent medicine for gaining access to my magic was? Willingness. I needed to be willing to change, willing to suffer, willing to let go, and willing to confront the shadows of my fear. And I had to be ready to love. It is not an easy task.

Whatever form of transportation you use, your willingness will lead you to your magic—and even allow you to share it with those you care about. I had an experience that accomplished exactly that around a year after the Holy Slap.

Several members of our family had long desired to hold a ceremony together, so I decided to plan an aya journey with facilitators who had been leading circles for nearly thirty years. They took a group of musicians with them who would play ceremonial music throughout the eight-hour trek on both nights, as well as help us. Will, as well as other members of my tribe, were present.

It had been a little more than eleven years since that first night in Ojai in the Medicine Woman's driveway, with me bearing little more than my fruit offering. I'd traveled a great distance.

Most of us were not new to ceremony, but it was our first time sharing it in a circle. What I liked about this idea was that it didn't matter where we were in our own journeys—on these nights, we'd each focus on our own self-discovery and healing while also holding space for one another by simply being there. In all of our lovely flaws, in all of our love for ourselves and each other.

I hadn't seen my panther in a long time, despite doing aya for many years. But this time she came back, and she walked her feline prowl beside me rather than in front of me, guiding me deeper into my inner world—perhaps as a preview of a new adventure to come. Some argue that the Black Panther is deformed because she is a cougar or jaguar with excessive pigmentation to mask her spots. However, a panther's so-called flaw is her very strength and beauty. The panther is a magician, transforming her flaws into amazing confidence, allowing her to stalk through the night's shadows unseen.

The panther is a protective guardian with keen vision, courage, and strength, as well as a sign of death and rebirth. Her magic includes assisting in the retrieval of light from the grips of shadow. I was relieved to see her again.

We all emerged from our final night of ceremony shining and bright, with full, open, and nourished hearts. I had a chance to look around at everyone—family and friends—just before we ended, and I thought about everything we had been through together and apart. All of our hardships, misunderstandings, and willingness to keep learning had led us to this moment of love.

Chet, who seemed to have lost eons over the previous two nights, caught my eye. I'd brought him out to L.A. when he'd returned from jail five years before, and here we were, together, from the hazardous streets of Baltimore and the days of sling'n drugs to doing a whole new level of "work" together. What a marvel. He had not wasted time in developing a program called Jefe Lifestyle to assist people in their quest to feel worthy and in control of their own lives. Then there was Mia, who had walked alongside me through many struggles since high school and was now seated with a calmness I had never seen in her. This was her first aya ceremony, and she soon told me, tearfully, that it had changed her life.

The magician in me looked around, and I saw the physical yet unseen golden threads of love joining everyone of us. Memories of people who had been so much a part of my life but were no longer physically present let me know that they had always held my hand. I looked across at Will and felt... differently as I began to cry from the overpowering emotion of loving and being really, deeply loved. Our tangled background didn't erase the undeniable fact that I couldn't reject our spiritual kinship.

He noticed I was ready to say something and waited.

"You are the King of my heart," I declared.

Will's eyes shone brightly, as if he was letting his heart to bloom unexpectedly. Then he told me that I was his heart's Queen. After a brief pause, he smiled and added, "You'll have to cut off your spirit's wrist to break free of our Divine handcuffs."

We both realized that these declarations were not romantic in character. This was not a fairy-tale finale, but a strong acknowledgment of a bond created in the midst of intense heat. And within that cauldron fire, we had burned away much of what no longer served us, allowing us to revel in the truth of what remained—unconditional love.

I was a Queen, and he was a King. I could feel my powerful contribution to the creation of this magnificent kingdom that I had gone long and hard to find—only to discover on the way that the kingdom had always been here. It offered me joy to bask in the glow that night with the folks I adore. I had everything I had been looking for just now.

We had been so focused on the outside, but suddenly we were more balanced and tuned in to the golden kingdom within us, between us, and within our family. And it was now ours to cultivate, in whatever shape it took.

If the grail is enough for you, Mr. Hero's Journey, I apologize. More is required for the heroine. The heroine is on a quest to find her kingdom of love. The Queen's power is the golden thread of love that she weaves throughout the kingdom, which grants her insight into the unseen world. She can hold many planets, many hearts, and many spirits at the same time, all while surrounding and offering her King love, sight, and wisdom. She stands behind him with her velvet sword, as I learned from Queen Afua, while he wields his steel sword, and they create their cosmos together. She is the hidden power that equals the strength of his visible might. It requires both of them to make life complete. (Note: When I use this comparison, don't think of King and Queen as gendered; instead, think of energy that you can pick.)

A Queen must journey in order to learn how to create a crown on her heart. How to grieve with her hands in the air, completely surrendered, praying with the Divine to keep her floating in her sea of tears and guide her path. How to find her torch in the deepest caverns of her anxieties, and how to write lullabies that soothe dragons to sleep. How to sew her heavenly shrouds with her own hands to tenderly defend her borders. How to summon the fortitude to search for the treasures concealed behind tender agony. How to remove the debris from her heart's wounds and let her tears and self-soothing to magically change everything to gold. She fashions her crown out of this gold. Her trip will last a lifetime, and she will continue to accumulate valuable stones of self-knowledge and Divine knowledge to place on her crown along the way. These diamonds open her heart's eyes. With these eyes, she knows she is lovable and worthwhile, as are all the souls she meets.

A Queen is her own rescuer. Her magic is subtle, forceful, and enigmatic.

My wish for you is that you comprehend that every step of your journey is leading you to your own crown. I hope you find your own magic, your own power, and your own self-love. My wish for you is to find the golden threads to weave the inner kingdom that will support the creation of your chosen existence. And may you use the golden threads you find to guide other heroines and heroes to and through their adventures.

Love and direction are always present for us, to guide us through the shadows of our hearts and valleys of our souls with the memory of our beauty and light—to help the bits of us that have been lost find their way home.